Praise for *Bypassing 'No' in*

"As a licensed Life Insurance Producer, I found *Bypassing 'No' in Business* to be a literal goldmine of new strategies for reducing and eliminating objections, selling more insurance and ultimately, putting more money in the bank!"
-**Mitchell Briegel,**
Licensed Insurance Agent, State Farm Insurance

"Authors Vincent Harris and Harlan Goerger are on top of their game in *ByPassing 'No' in Business*. They use interesting and entertaining case studies and examples to show how you can succeed in sales. The best part: their ideas are immediately actionable. Read the book today. Start bypassing 'No' tomorrow. The chapters on decision points and saying "No" to the customer to get a "Yes" are worth the price of the book alone. Based on solid research, yet practical in its application, this is a must-read book for anyone in sales—which is all of us."
-**Vicki Kunkel, Author of** *Instant Appeal: The 8 Primal Factors that Create Blockbuster Success.*

"What does it take to be maximally effective in influencing people so that they will be receptive to what you are offering? Vincent Harris and Harlan Goerger reveal the secrets to powerfully influencing others in their book, *Bypassing 'No' in Business*. If you are ready to learn the secrets to achieving success, this is the book for you."
-**Dr. Joe Rubino, CEO,**
http://www.CenterForPersonalReinvention.com
Creator, http://TheSelfEsteemBook.com

"Exactly what I needed! This book is practical. I knew I was obtaining thousands of dollars of advice for the low price of this powerful book. As a business coach I look forward to recommending this book to my clients and watching their incomes and quality of life soar. This book is a 'must read.'"
**-Dr. Clare Albright, Author of *Neurofeedback: Transforming Your Life with Brain Biofeedback*,
http://www.DrClarity.com**

"Bypassing 'No' is more than converting the response to "Yes"; it is creating rapport. Learn from Harlan and Vincent how to completely dissolve resistance. Stimulating examples for practical application—you'll even learn what it means when a wolf smiles! You need this book; I am confident you will benefit from these powerful new tactics for Bypassing 'No.' The amazing knowledge is presented in an engaging style that makes it easy to absorb and immediately put into practice.
**Lyle R. Johnson, Ph.D., MBA, President,
L R Johnson, Inc.**

"This is a real gem of a book full of practical and thought provoking ideas and stories; very rarely do you come across the combination of sales techniques and body language in such a powerful way. A must read for all sales professionals or anyone interested in the power of influence"
**Cillian O'Grady,
Senior Director Business Development Group,
Oracle Direct EMEA**

"Principles, Tactics and Harnessing the Power of Communication wait for you as you drink in the wisdom of getting past "no" on every page of this book. Riveting at times, thought provoking at others. An excellent addition to your persuasion library."
Kevin Hogan, Author, *The Psychology of Persuasion*

Goerger and Harris didn't set out to impress you with how much they know about sales and influence (and they know a lot!). Instead, they focus on showing *you* exactly how to use practical strategies to get to "YES" with greater ease than ever before. A powerful toolbox for anyone who wants to lead others to win-win solutions."
-Dr. Mollie Marti,
Author of *The 12 Factors of Business Success,*
Founder of http://wwwBestLifeDesign.com

About the Authors
Harlan Goerger

Harlan Goerger is the "Different Thinking" guy. His programs such as the Advanced Sales Program and Leadership Strategies provide a different look at sales, leadership and communications. As a three time author Harlan has put his different thinking in the hands of thousands of business people and the results, up to 400% growth, show the ideas work!

The quick story, as a twelve year old farm boy he was given 250 head of hogs to raise and make money for the family. Always up for a challenge he later grew the family agriculture business some 400%, including an export branch. With the loss of a wonderful wife at age 29, he found himself a single dad of 3, with one in diapers. To provide the income and time to raise a family he pursued a career with Dale Carnegie Training and shortly became a regional manager, developing his own sales and training team. But as always, wanting more challenges and ideas, Harlan struck out on his own consulting and training ideas.

Today Harlan operates CEO Solutions programs for business owners, operates with growing businesses on a retainer basis and coaches both executives and individuals on breaking barriers. His specialty areas are Sales and Leadership Development.

About the Authors
Vincent Harris, M.S.

An internationally recognized expert on body language, peak performance, and non-verbal communication, Vincent Harris is often referred to as **"America's Body Language Guy"**. Author of *The Productivity Epiphany*, hundreds of articles, and the audio series, *Secrets for Getting Things Done*, he is also a speaker and seminar leader, consultant, and one-on-one coach.

He is also regularly called on by the media, including NBC, MTV, and Fox News to do **Celebrity Body Language Analysis**. Some of his recent analyses include the Tiger Woods Apology and Press Conference, the David Arquette Oprah interview, the Jay Leno Oprah Interview, and the "After the Rose" Bachelor episode.

Drawing from his undergraduate degree in education, his graduate degree in psychology, and continuous study of memory, neurology, and the latest research on adult learning strategies, Vince coaches individuals on how to deal with pain; alter physiology to deal with stress and access peak performance; eliminate procrastination and get things done; and read others' body language for success in sales and in life!

Bypassing 'No' In Business

Bypassing 'No' in Business
Copyright © 2010 by Harlan Goerger and Vincent Harris
ISBN: 978-0-9818791-9-2

Beckworth Publications
3108 E 10th St
Trenton, Mo 64683

Beckworth Publications and the Beckworth Publications logo are trademarks of Beckworth Publications.

Printed in the United States of America.

Library of Congress Cataloging-in-Publication Data.

Goerger, Harlan, and Harris, Vincent
Bypassing 'No' in Business: Selling Your Ideas with Ease;
New Body Language and Influence Strategies to Eliminate or Reduce Resistance to Just about Anything.

Library of Congress Control Number: 2010910817

Copyediting and proofreading by Jean Boles and Coleen Gunn
Book cover design by Mike Baugher
Interior Design by Jean Boles

Bypassing 'No' in Business:

Selling Your Ideas with Ease

*New Body Language and Influence Strategies
to Eliminate or Reduce Resistance
to Just about Anything.*

by

Harlan Goerger & Vincent Harris

Table of Contents

Table of Contents

FOREWORD

Why you should say "Yes" to this Book

Let me restate that point! When a persuader encounters, or is likely to encounter resistance, the most effective persuasion strategies are those aimed at deactivating the "No" part of the evaluation. Bypassing the "No" is the focus of this book. And this is a great book. The next 30 chapters explain in simple, concrete ways more than 30 things you can do to bypass the "No" part of a customer's evaluation.

You will see that these influence strategies work in various ways. Some of these work by lowering the customer's need to evaluate or look for hazards. Others work by directly addressing the "cons" or costs that a customer might raise. Others work by focusing the resistance on a particular issue or time. These 30 chapters provide quite an arsenal for the persuader. These influence strategies reduce the customer's resistance, thereby freeing them to consider the opportunities and benefits of your offer.

You will really like a number of things about these chapters. First, the strategies they describe are useful and effective. They really work. Second, they are novel, not yet part of most persuaders' tool kits. Because of these first two reasons, you will find many things in these chapters that will justify and return many-fold the price of this book. Third, the techniques are clearly and simply described and include wonderfully illustrative examples.

Each chapter gives you a clear picture of what to do. Practice the technique for a short time and you will have a wonderful tool with which to expand your tool kit. Finally, these effective techniques work with little or no cost to the persuader. Your presentations aren't going to take longer. You won't have to lower the price or add incentives or bundle products in order to reduce resistance. These techniques work without reducing your margin. I like that a lot. So will you.

So, try a little bit of this book. If you find this little bit useful, then be glad that you still have the rest of the book to go. If you don't find the first several chapters useful, then be glad you have only spent a little time and money to find out how smart and well-equipped you are. In either case, this book will have a positive influence on you and make you a better persuader.

"No" is a negative word in more ways than one. It is unpleasant to hear; it is distasteful to utter. It implies that someone's understanding is being denied, or that someone's goal is being thwarted. It's a word that separates us, rather than joins us. In addition, "No" is a difficult word.

For even the simplest of questions, "No" answers take longer to formulate than "Yes" answers. It seems that more cognitive work is being put into a "No" answer.

The bottom line, of course, is that for an advocate, a salesperson, a manager, or just about anyone else, hearing the word "No" in response to a request or offer signifies failure, and that is personally and interpersonally negative.

"No" and "Yes" in the Brain

"No," of course, is necessary. Life would be unworkable without it. "No" is the Yang to "Yes's" Yin. In fact, our brain was built with this duality of mind. We know from psychology and neuroscience that people scan and evaluate the environment through two separate brain pathways simultaneously.

Bypassing 'No' In Business

The Behavioral Activation System (BAS) is a set of structures and pathways that are attuned to perceiving and evaluating the opportunities in the environment and to motivating the person to approach those opportunities. Different desires make us attuned to different aspects of the environment.

A thirsty person notices each water fountain along the corridor, discerns the path to get there, and, almost tasting the water, feels the urge to move to each fountain. The BAS, essentially, is the "Yes" system, structured to get us what we want to have.

At the same time, a separate set of structures and pathways, called the Behavioral Inhibition System, or BIS, operates to notice and evaluate the hazards and pitfalls in the environment and motivates the person to avoid these dangers.

The BIS is attuned to the signs of threat or danger in the environment. It is the BIS that identifies the rust or signs of soiling around the water fountain, raises a concern about turning one's back to take a drink. It evaluates the seriousness and potency of potential threats and stands ready to inhibit action that would bring one closer to a threat. The BIS, essentially, is the "No" system, structured to help us avoid what we want to not have.

How does someone decide, for instance, whether to take a drink from a water fountain? The decision maker in our brain integrates the information and assessments from these two pathways, weighs strengths of the motives against the opportunities and dangers and decides the best course of action. This cost-benefit analysis is actually well known, well understood, and well practiced by most people, including advocates, salespeople, managers, and other persuaders.

What is not fully appreciated is how separate the BIS and the BAS pathways are, and how this separateness can impact persuasion. I'm sure as I described the BIS and the BAS in the paragraphs above, you were able to think of people who personify one orientation but not the other. Someone with a dominant Activation System, but a weak Inhibition System, would be an unbridled optimist. This is the person who jumps without knowing where he or she will land. This person tends to be need-driven, impulsive, given to immediate gratification, often getting in trouble by neglecting warning signs.

The opposite person, someone with an overly strong Inhibition System and a weak Activation System, would be an unbridled pessimist. This is someone who is skeptical about any opportunity, looks for exceptions to the rule, expresses contrary opinions and uses the word "but" frequently; this is the person who often can't make up his or her mind because there is always another downside to consider. In the end, this person has a constricted life, inhibited from taking any action.

Ever encounter people like this? Of course you have. However, the important point is not that these two systems define different types of people. No, the important point is that they describe two parts of you and two parts of everyone. Each system is hard-wired into each person's brain and neurochemistry.

So when you present your great idea, your wonderful deal, your best proposal, know that it becomes available to be evaluated by both the "Yes" system and the "No" system of the recipient. What are the implications of this duality?

No and Yes in Persuasion

Most people assume that the persuader's task is to provide the target of persuasion with enough reasons to move from saying "No" to saying "Yes." They think of people as weighing the pros and cons of an offer or opportunity as on a scale. When persuaders meet resistance, usually the first thought is to refine the rhetoric, explaining more clearly and more forcefully the reasons for saying "Yes." If more or better reasons don't work, then persuaders typically think next of ways to "sweeten" the offer, by discounting the cost, or bundling it with additional features.

Both potential strategies may increase the likelihood of a "Yes," but both also have strong downsides. Refining the argument, in addition to sounding defensive, is likely to raise more resistance. The persuader pushing harder makes the customer feel like pushing back harder. Sweetening the deal is a costly alternative. It cuts into the margin, often deeply ("I'm losing just a little on each sale, but the volume is way up!") And, if either of these strategies does happen to produce a "Yes" answer, they produce an ambivalent "Yes." The "Yes" is ambivalent because the customer's concerns still remain. They haven't been diminished.

The scale with pros and cons is actually an accurate and useful analogy. The dual mental processes involved in assessing a situation mean that the "Yes" system of the brain is adding to the pros side of the scale at the same time that the "No" system is adding to the con side of the scale. Visualize this scale. You can clearly see that the persuader's best strategy is to reduce the con side of the scale, rather than adding to the pro side.

When a customer is teetering between a "Yes" and a "No," if the persuader can deactivate or remove some of the cons, then the choice falls naturally toward "Yes," without the persuader adding more incentives or more reasons for saying "Yes." And, the customer feels less ambivalence, less remorse, about the "Yes." With less ambivalence, there is less post-decision remorse and less rumination about what might have been. The customer is more comfortable with the decision and more confident in taking action based on that choice.

Most salespeople, advisers, or other persuaders don't make an offer without knowing that it has a lot of favorable features—features that make it attractive to potential customers. Given the fact that you've got a good product, the secret to promoting and producing acceptance of that product, I think, is to focus on the cons and make them go away.

Chapter 1:
Bypassing "No" vs. Overcoming "No"

"The secret of my influence has always been that it remained secret."

-Salvador Dali

As an insurance salesperson—nearly a quarter of a century ago—I was repeatedly told, *"The average person will say no seven times before they say yes. Just hang in there, keep closing, and you'll sell a lot of insurance!"*

Even at the age of twenty, without knowing too much about anything, something about this seemed out of whack. I knew, for example, that when I went into a store to look at the latest Van Halen album (yes, it was a long time ago), I was not compelled to say no seven times—not even one time. They had it, asked if I wanted it, and I said "Yes!"

Some would argue: *"But that's a small ticket item—it's not the same with more expensive stuff!"* In 1986, I bought a new Chevy S-10 Blazer for $18,789. That was a whole lot of dough in 1986. Did I say no seven times before signing the papers and driving away? Not a chance. I found the red and black beauty I wanted and bought it. Do you see the pattern? I wanted it...so I said "YES!"—the *first* time.

Action:

I bailed out of selling insurance door-to-door after about a year. I was cold calling, and most of the people I was talking to (read that as ALL of the people) did not *want* to buy insurance; let's forget about whether they *needed* it and focus on the fact that they did not *want* it. Those who did buy from me did so because they liked me—a lot. (I will explain why they liked me later, when we get into the chapters on body language and non-verbal communication.)

I was not willing then, or now, to barrel through seven no's, and strong-arm someone into buying something they did not want. If I am on the other end of things, after about the second "No," I start getting testy. Long before getting to the seventh "No," I would be moving them *away* from me. I do not like it when it's happening to me, and I will not do it to someone else. It is irritating, plain and simple.

> **"I was not willing, then, or now, to barrel through seven "no's" to strong arm someone into buying something they had asserted seven times that they didn't want."**

When it comes to sales, the key is only talking to people who have an interest in what you are selling. When you do that, you are half-way home. However, when it comes to selling to people that you work with everyday, well, you deal with the people you have to deal with; no niche marketing to save you here.

The Change:

My life changed dramatically when I started combining my unconsciously developed gift for bonding deeply with the people I decided to bond with and the consciously adopted skills of influence; specifically, body language, non-verbal communication, and proven verbal patterns for reducing resistance *before* it ever had a chance to manifest.

You won't have to use what you learn in this book to go out and make a million-dollar deal to feel like you got more than your money's worth. Say for example, you suggest movie 'A,' and they say "No," you are in a bartering dance of sorts. You have to overcome "No" just to get them back to their baseline. Then, by saying something like: *"I'll (insert unwanted task) if you go to movie 'A'..."* you attempt to cajole them into 'Yes.'

Of course, there are an endless number of similar situations that will occur. Try being a manager who has to present a change requested by upper management to a group of already overwhelmed and stressed employees. I don't think I have to tell you what you'll be up against once the group has had a chance to adopt a "No" attitude.

However you want to look at it, most people will find life far more enjoyable when the number of "No's" they are hearing decrease radically. That is exactly what this book will teach you to do.

Reality:

Am I suggesting that by using what you learn in this book, you will never hear people say "No" to you? Let me ask you a question; would it be okay if you could just cut the frequency of "No's" in half? If you were thinking, "YES!" then hang on, because you are in for a ride that will bestow you with the skills that enable you to do just that. This book gives you the most state-of-the-art tools for "Bypassing No" you can find. If you choose to use them, these tools will bring rewards you might not even be able to imagine—yet.

Bypassing 'No' In Business

Chapter 2:
Avoiding Body Language Overload

"At the end of reasons comes persuasion."

-Ludwig Wittgenstein

Body language is a crucial factor for "Bypassing No." Not only the body language and non-verbal cues that you detect and decipher in others, but the signals that you generate and transmit yourself. After all, this is a two-way street, and you are half the traffic.

Human consciousness is very limited. We can only keep track of a few separate pieces of information at any given time. Once we go over the threshold, our awareness becomes saturated, and from that point on, we are pretty much missing everything.

I have witnessed people so focused on reading someone's body language—for detecting deception—that they completely missed one verbal slip-up after another.

Overload:

If I want someone to ignore blue cars on the highway, I am not going to tell them to forget about the blue cars (this actually emphasizes them). I am going to ask them to count all of the red, green and white cars. By clogging their awareness with red, green and white, they will likely delete the blue cars from their consciousness without any overt request or instructions on my part.

Many people who embark on a path to become skilled at reading body language do the same thing to themselves. By trying to track too many body language signals at once, they preclude themselves from noticing other critical information.

How We Learn:

Remember what it was like when you first learned to drive? Every move you made, from flipping on the turn signal, to looking in the rear-view mirror, required a massive hunk of your limited awareness.

In time, though, most of those behaviors became automatic and no longer required you to focus on them consciously. Once this happened, it freed your conscious awareness for other things.

Pick one aspect of body language to master at a time. You might start with paying attention to voice qualities, things like volume, pitch, intonation etc. Then, after this becomes a natural and automatic action for you, simply shift to another area, like facial expressions.

The Example:

I like the story of the guy who was going to use body language to determine if his wife wanted to go to a movie. After asking, *"Honey, do you want to go see a show?"* he carefully watched for any signs that would reveal her answer. His intensity was incredible. Finally, after what seemed like a lifetime, his wife said, *"Forget it then!"* and stormed out of the room.

She had been saying "Yes" for two to three minutes, but because he was so focused on her non-verbal communication, he simply did not notice she was speaking. This, my friends, is the "Body Language Death Blow"—avoid it!

Do you know—*really* know—how you ride a bike? In case you don't know the answer to that question, it's "No, you don't!" If you can ride, you simply jump on and go; you don't think about what each leg should do and when and how many degrees your torso should lean to make sure you stay upright and move forward.

Thinking back, you know there *was* a time when you were trying desperately to track all of these things at once, and you likely crashed and burned several times in the process. (Ouch, so many skinned knees!) Unfortunately, when it comes to learning to ride a bike, you do not get to learn one aspect at a time; it is all or nothing.

The Plan:

Happily, you DO get the opportunity to master body language and non-verbal communication one chunk at a time, and I would invite you to progress in this manner.

Once you can single out and mimic the breathing patterns of others (and yourself), it becomes as automatic as flipping on the turn signal while driving. After you have achieved automaticity with breathing patterns, for example, you can then do the same with facial expressions, gestures, postures, muscle tension, etc.

Using this one-chunk-at-a-time strategy will allow you to reach a point of unconscious competence, and this is critical, otherwise, you'll be using so much of your limited awareness that you miss the blatant and obvious "YES!" that a client or customer is communicating.

In short, there are people who do not know about body language; people who do know about body language; and there are those who are "masters" of body language. The latter are rare, not because it is difficult to achieve, but because most people never employ a progressive system for automation at the unconscious level. You can; and when you do, you will be rewarded handsomely and "Bypass No" frequently.

The journey of a thousand miles starts with one step; you can always take one more step, and when you do, a new world will slowly—or quickly—reveal itself to you.

IMPORTANT: When it comes to business, sales and influence, what YOU do with your OWN body language will have far more impact than what you might see others doing with their body language

Chapter: 3
How to Use a Twenty-Dollar Bill to Stay Focused and Resilient

"I have a resistance to change in things that I feel comfortable with and that I'm used to."

-Dennis Quaid

"Bypassing No" can often require a fair amount of patience. Patience is a derivative of the stressors present in a given situation divided by your ability to stay relaxed, resourceful and focused. While a million and one techniques for doing this are floating around, it often comes down to perspective, or, in other words, a mindset.

Putting the "stressful" events of your life in perspective may just be a $20 bill away. No, it's not something you can purchase with the $20, but something you can experience from looking at the gentleman on the front, Andrew Jackson.

Symbol Power:

Simple symbols or images can trigger powerful feelings and resources within us. As a United States Navy veteran, looking at the flag during the National Anthem makes the hair on my arms stand on end, and various religious symbols can initiate a strong cascade of feelings and emotions in those who practice a particular faith.

The image of Andrew Jackson found on the $20 bill can trigger a similar response, once you become aware of the man behind the image.

The Story:

Jackson came into the world just weeks after his father was killed in a logging accident. At the age of 13, Andrew, and his older brother, Robert, became couriers in the revolutionary war by joining the local regiment. Shortly thereafter, both boys were captured by British soldiers. They were barely given enough food to sustain life.

While captive, the Jackson brothers contracted small pox, and this, combined with the near starvation conditions, had both boys hovering near death's door.

Their mother successfully made a case for their release; she hammered on the fact that they were just children, and eventually, their release was arranged.

When she arrived to bring them home, she draped Robert, who was the sickest, over the only horse she had. She and Andrew (who was just about as ill) walked the 40 miles back home. His mother led the horse as Andrew stumbled along behind it.

Shortly after arriving home, Robert died from his weakened condition. Andrew's mother assured him that he would be fine, and she left home to care for wounded soldiers.

Within months, she too, died from small pox, and at the age of 14, Andrew Jackson was an orphan. His father, his mother, brother Robert, and an older brother, Hugh, (who succumbed to heat exhaustion while a soldier) were all dead and gone.

Fast forward a few years. Andrew Jackson became a lawyer; he was elected the first US Representative in Tennessee; he was later elected US

Senator and judge of the Tennessee Supreme Court; he was a decorated military leader; and he became the seventh President of the United States.

A quite impressive list of accomplishments; he had finally reached a point where the turmoil was over, right? Not quite. Just two months before he took the office of President, his wife Rachael died of a heart attack. For most of his life, Jackson would periodically cough up blood because of a musket ball that had lodged near his heart when he was shot during one of the many duels he had fought over the years.

In 1845, Andrew Jackson died at the age of 78 from tuberculosis and heart failure; a tremendous age considering that most men of this period died prior to the age of 50.

Andrew Jackson had every reason in the world to give up on life. He could have said, "My father died before I was born, both my mother and a brother died of small pox, and another brother died while fighting in the war. I've had a horrible life. I'm emotionally scarred and will never be able to have any kind of stability in my life!" He could have taken that path—but he didn't.

Jackson held the leadership positions that he did, perhaps, because of his previous experiences.

The Point:

So, the next time you are feeling like the world is against you, that you have been knocked down too many times to make it out of your current conditions, look at the face on the $20 bill. He was also knocked down, but he picked himself up every time.

Trying one of the techniques in this book may not always go as smoothly as you would like in the beginning, but if you have the resilience of Jackson, by the second or third try you will see dividends!

Another bonus that comes with resilience is self-confidence; you'll become a calm observant communicator who sees what others miss.

The techniques for "Bypassing No," coupled with a resilient and resourceful attitude will find you hearing "YES" more often, and most likely, putting more of Jackson's twenties in the bank.

Body Language Take Away: Take the Fast Lane to Resilience

Every mental and emotional state has a corresponding body language "recipe." People who are feeling resilient breathe differently than people who are feeling depressed. For example, they gesture, nod, speak, move— EVERYTHING—differently than someone in a different state or emotion.

Do you want to feel resilient anytime, anywhere, regardless of the circumstances? You can!

Get a notebook for this exercise to reap the maximum benefit. Imagine you are going to star in a movie. You will be playing the role of the most resilient person on earth. You will be paid one million dollars for the role if you successfully pull off acting resilient. If you were going to act resilient, what changes would you make? Whatever they are, start making a detailed list in your notebook.

Answer the following questions in detail:

- How would you breathe?
- How would you gesture?
- How would you stand?
- How would you sit?
- What facial expressions would you have?
- What would your voice tone sound like?

- What would happen to the speed of your voice (both externally and for your inner dialogue)?
- What would happen to your muscle tension (more or less)?

If you knew the one million dollars would be all yours if you could pull it off, would it be worth spending fifteen minutes a day rehearsing resilience, using the answers you wrote down to the questions above to guide you? Of course you would. However, you are not likely in that situation, so let me ask you another question.

Would it be useful to be able to maintain your composure and stay focused through whatever life throws at you?

When you can keep a cool head and your mind on important tasks when everyone around you is running around like a chicken with its head cut off, you will be able to capitalize on opportunities others miss. In addition, this could be worth far more than a million dollars in the long run—maybe even the short run.

For twenty bucks, most anyone could instantly access a state of frustration or anger. Most, however, would fail miserably at instantly accessing resilience, calmness or an "in-the-zone" focus. Why? It's quite simple; most people have had LOTS of practice getting mad or frustrated; they have rehearsed it hundreds, if not thousands, of times. Therefore, it is easy and automatic.

If you want to access states that are more resourceful for "Bypassing No," you will find it useful to begin methodically rehearsing states like resilience. Like any skilled actor, the more you rehearse, the better you will be. As Milton Erickson said, *"You can pretend anything until you master it!"*

Bypassing 'No' In Business

Chapter 4:
Myth Busting & Body Language

*"Electric communication will never be a substitute for
the face of someone who with their soul encourages
another person to be brave and true."*

-Charles Dickens

Almost everyone has heard about the famous study conducted at Yale many years ago where they followed the students who had written specific goals, and twenty years later, found that this 3% had accumulated more wealth than the 97% that had not written specific goals. Impressive, right? There is one little problem though, it is an urban legend! Myths like these cannot only survive for years, but many of them continue to get stronger.

Albert Mehrabian's findings regarding non-verbal communication have been butchered so badly they almost rival the Yale myth.

Myth Busting:

When meeting new people someone will usually ask me, *"What do you do?"* After telling them I am an author, speaker and consultant, the "body language expert" thing comes up somewhere in the conversation.

Most times, they will proudly say, *"Oh, yes...I know about that; 93% of our communication is non-verbal and only 7% of our communications' effectiveness is the words!"* Of course, they have no idea how preposterous that is. If they were to actually think about it—but most people just see or hear something and then accept it or reject it—they don't think about it, at least not critically.

To help them get past their misinterpretation of Mehrabian's hard work and research, I ask them to do a little role playing with me. I take out a napkin and write: *There are 16 screws on the back of my stereo speakers that have to be removed before the cone can be properly inspected.* I make sure they cannot see what I am writing, and then I fold it up.

"Okay, I'm going to communicate my message to you—the one I have written down—using only non-verbal communication, and then I want you to tell me what my message was." I then go through a series of exaggerated facial expressions, gestures, and make sounds within my throat that go up and down in pitch and volume. *"Now, what was my message?"*

I am usually met with laughter, sometimes by silence, and other times by massive confusion. *"Oh, here let me try again,"* I say, and then I change my facial expressions and the sound of my voice. *"Got it now?"*

Clearly, NO ONE EVER gets anywhere close to decoding my message. After they have finally said, *"I have no idea what you wrote down,"* I'll ask, *"Didn't you say that 93% of the effectiveness of our communication was non-verbal? If that's the case, you should be able to get pretty close just by watching and listening to my non-verbal communication, right?"*

Next, I slowly open up the napkin, and in my slowest, most monotone voice, without any physical movement, I read, *"There are 16 screws on the back of my stereo speakers that have to be removed before the cone can be properly inspected."* I then ask, *"Now, what was my message?"* They quickly and easily repeat my message.

"Sometimes, the words we use can be EVERYTHING!" I tell them with conviction.

The Truth:

Mehrabian was saying that when the words we are using are not in accord with the non-verbal communication we are using, the listener has a tendency to believe the non-verbal communication.

If someone says, *"Oh yes, I love you!"* with a look of contempt on their face (the only emotion with an asymmetrical facial expression), we may respond with *"Screw you too!"* Yes, their words were saying one thing, but their non-verbal signals are saying another, and, by default, we choose the non-verbal signals as the "truth."

A key point in "Bypassing No" is to be aware of your body language when talking about any type of emotional issue. Be sure both the words and your body (and facial) language are in accord!

The next time someone cranks out the Yale story (sometimes they use Harvard), or pulls the *"93% of communication is non verbal"* line on you, just stop, and say, *"yes, interesting,"* and then change the subject.

Bypassing 'No' In Business

Chapter 5:
The Most Important Principle

"You gotta know when to hold'em, know when to fold'em..."

-Kenny Rogers, The Gambler

I , Vincent Harris, (V.H.) do a lot of work with clients one-on-one. Some of them meet with me in person, but over the years, I have shifted to doing more of my work over the telephone. Because I live in North Central Missouri, working with clients residing in places like Poland, Hong Kong, Guam and the U.K., means that sometimes, face-to-face simply isn't an option. Today, 80% of my clients are business people looking to either make a breakthrough, earn more money, or learn to communicate more effectively, Ten years ago, almost all of my clients were in "corrective" situations; they had chronic pain issues, bad habits interfering with their health or life, anxiety, phobias, or were extremely overweight. In other words, they saw themselves as being "broken," and much like humpty dumpty, they were looking for me to put them back together again.

The Ah-Ha:

My remedial clients taught me the importance of creating, and holding fast, to certain "rules" about my work, and more specifically, with whom I was willing to work as a client.

As a social scientist, I often use the term *secondary gain* to describe the phenomenon of someone not making a change that, from everyone else's perspective, is the only logical choice. One that would be beneficial for them to make, yet they do NOT make the change. Actually, they appear to work very hard to keep change from happening.

I first encountered this while helping clients with chronic pain. Gradually, a pattern started to emerge, and I made a rule—that I live by—to only channel my energy to those who would benefit most.

I discovered that once someone was granted full disability—regardless of their age—it was very likely that they were going to sabotage every effort made to increase their level of comfort. Most of them would never allow a complete resolution of their painful existence to occur.

Keep in mind, these were people who had called me to help them eliminate or reduce their pain. On one level, they did desire to get back to a pain-free life, but on another, far more influential level, they did not want to risk losing the financial compensation of disability payments they had worked so long and hard to get. This had become their new "comfort zone" even though it was painful.

The Action:

The rule I adopted, and one that I have adhered to ever since (with the exception of a few cases where I forgot to ask) is, I will not work with anyone on full disability—period!

Without the interference and inner conflict created by a financial gain (disability payments), I've had clients who were no longer responding well to morphine achieve a significant level of comfort by following my instructions on how to influence their nervous system. The outcome of my work was far more consistent, and the effort I had to expend was considerably less. Living by that one rule eliminated a great deal of frustration from my life.

What does this have to do with "Bypassing No" and getting to "Yes!"? EVERYTHING!

Reality:

If you sell cars, you will learn to "Bypass No" with people who are in the market for a car and are considering trading or buying. If you sell air conditioning units, you will learn to "Bypass No" with people who live where it gets hot enough to need one for at least part of the year.

What you will not learn is how to "Bypass No" and sell an air conditioner to someone living in the Antarctic; someone might be *able* to, but this doesn't make them a good salesperson, it makes them an un-ethical idiot. You need to develop rules about who is, and who is not, your client or customer. Then, you need to make sure you find out, in the beginning, which category the person you are talking to fits in. This will save you a great deal of time, and allow you to "Bypass No" more frequently with the right people. In sales and persuasion training, we call this "Qualifying."

Example:

Let me give you an example from my own life. I (V.H.) am 44 years old and have never owned a home. Furthermore, I never *want* to own a home, and almost certainly never will. My number one value in life is *freedom*, and the thought of being tied down to one geographical location, and being responsible for all of the maintenance, upkeep, etc. that goes with owning a home is about as appealing to me as watching paint dry on a humid August day in North Central Missouri.

For the last six years, I have lived on a beautiful 400-acre farm that belongs to a family who only frequents the property two-to-three times a year. There is a large, 3-bedroom farmhouse, a barn, a 90-foot trailer, a garage, a guesthouse where a farm hand lived during World War II, and a 90 x 60 foot Morton steel building. I have use of them all. This is where I am raising my daughter and have raised countless chickens, kittens, goats and my three faithful dogs, Katie, Bubbie and Ace. You couldn't interest me in owning a house for all of the tea in China.

If you sell houses, you could show me a house worth $295,000 that I could buy for $65,000, and I could care less. I do not want, and would not be interested in, owning a house—at any price. *"But Vince,"* you might say, *"You could just buy it and sell it for a tremendous profit!"* Still no interest. I make my money doing only things I enjoy doing, and the thought of buying the house and putting it on the market, etc. is not something I would enjoy doing. My point? You would be wasting your time with me and unable to "Bypass No."

If you had a rule that said: *I will only discuss the house with people who have expressed an interest in moving, buying a house, or are looking to use real estate for investment purposes,* you could then quickly and easily weed out the wrong people. You could spend your time talking to the right people, and THIS is where you will use your methods for "Bypassing No."

Before you begin taking the techniques and strategies you learn in this book and putting them into play, I would invite you to spend as much time as you need figuring out precisely who your client or customer is NOT. Many people go the other direction: they focus on identifying who their customer is, but somehow, this does not prevent them from letting people who clearly are NOT their ideal clients slip through and wasting a massive amount of their time.

The best strategy would be to spend time identifying both who is your customer or client, and who is NOT. When you can rapidly, and thoroughly, sort them out you can effectively employ the strategies for "Bypassing No."

Mental Clarity Exercise:

- Who is NOT your client or customer?
- Who do you NOT enjoy working with?
- What type of person usually does NOT buy your product or service?
- What "Rule" would save you time, energy and effort by keeping you more focused on doing what you should and NOT doing what you should not?

Do you have to stop and write the answers to these questions out on paper? Of course not, but if you write them out, and really think about the answers, the exercise will have a stronger impact.

Bypassing 'No' In Business

Chapter 6:
The Power of Liz

*How the Implicit Mind Directs Us

"Every extension of knowledge arises from making conscious the unconscious."

-Friedrich Nietzsche

Whenever there is a discussion about persuasion, influence or body language, there is one very important key element that most people either do not understand or completely miss.

When one understands this secret, many of the seemingly mystical behaviors of others become clear!

We start with a quick primer on how the brain is put together. This is over simplified, but we are not talking brain surgery, so no need for twelve-syllable names.

The Brain:

There are three parts to the brain. The most inner brain runs our body without our awareness. This part keeps our heart beating, lungs breathing and our body moving, all without our input or control.

The second part of the brain is our "primitive" brain. We share the first and second brain parts with our animal, insect and reptilian friends. This second part of the brain is a key element in influence and body language.

The third part is our cortex or upper and outer brain. This is the reasoning and thinking part of the brain. When we have a problem, we can process the inputs and come up with creative solutions. This is what makes us different from our animal and reptilian friends.

Why is the second part of our brain so important to persuasion and body language? Our animal and reptilian friends are dependent upon reaction to their current environment. They do very little to plan for tomorrow or prepare for future events. Because they lack the problem-solving cortex, they are mostly reactionary and instinctual in their behaviors.

Although the second level brain has seven different parts, for our purpose we will view it as one.

Inputs:

All inputs come to this primitive brain first. What you see, hear, feel and smell first goes through the primitive brain before the outer third level cortex gets the inputs. That is why you jump at a sudden noise only to realize it was nothing a moment later. Your primitive brain reacted before your logical thinking cortex kicked in. Scientists tell us there is a one-quarter to half-second delay in transmitting between the primitive brain and the cortex, thus the jumping at hearing a noise—jumping that is seemingly instantaneous.

This second-level primitive lizard brain (we will call this "Liz" for short) is always in a safe, fight/flight mode, always on the lookout for danger so the lizard can continue to survive.

Sensing anything that might be of danger, "Liz," determines if we should fight or run. Watch a house cat explore a new territory as it cautiously sniffs paws and tenses its body. The cat is in fight/flight mode.

Because all of our external inputs come through "Liz," we are in this fight/flight mode as well. When we meet a new person, "Liz" is scanning for movements, smells, feelings that help determine if this is a safe person or an enemy.

How "Liz" Works:

If "Liz" does not think or reason, how does "Liz" know how to react?

Have you ever seen a coin sorter? You put a hand full of coins in the machine and it sorts them by pennies, nickels, dimes and quarters. There is no thought to this, a coin either fits in a slot or it doesn't.

An infant is hungry and gives out a cry. A bottle shows up and the hunger goes away. A reaction "coin slot" is created from "cry = gets food." Each experience we have in life either creates a new "reaction slot" or reinforces an existing one. "Liz" uses these "slots" to determine safe-fight/flight reactions.

A smile means safe and secure and fits a safe slot. Without us even thinking about it, we smile back and both of us feel safe. *(By the way, a smile is actually a submission signal, which is why it is so disarming to others. A wolf, for example, that appears to be smiling, is actually showing submission to other, more dominant wolves. The Alpha wolf will almost never "smile." By smiling, the wolf avoids a fight with a larger, more powerful wolf, and human beings get to "Bypass No!")*

A frown or scowl means danger, and thus, fits a danger slot. We feel uncomfortable and may not even know why, but we become cautious. Cautious can quickly equal "No."

Take a child who was constantly being slapped. A reactionary slot is formed which instructs: "raised hand is pain." This child grows up and is in a meeting.

The presenter constantly raises his hand up in the air and swings it down like a slap. The adult does not like this person or anything they are saying or presenting and feels very uncomfortable but does not know why! "Liz" is reacting to "raised hand is pain!" The cortex never gets this message unless the adult starts questioning why and digs out the reactionary slot!

Because everything we see, hear, taste, smell or touch goes through "Liz" first, we have very little control during that quarter to half-second delay before the "Thinking Cortex" takes over.

Out of Control:

If you have ever experienced, or seen, total fear or extreme anger turned to rage, you have experienced a "short circuiting" of the "Liz" to cortex connection. "Liz" is now 100% in control and completely reactionary in fight/flight mode. (In my youth, another young man almost went to the hospital because my "Liz" was in control.) You thought you were always in control—Not!

Body Language & Influence:

So on to body language and influence. That first half a second of meeting a new person has "Liz" making a judgment; in what slot do you fit? Safe or danger is the outcome before any thought has been put into the choice. Thus, anything we can do to provide the safest impression immediately upon meeting someone will pay us the most dividends. Later, our actions, words and tone will either reinforce the safe choice or cause it to swing to danger. All of this happens with 99% of people being completely unaware of why, or how, these feelings occur.

You now understand why first impressions are so important and how people can say, *"I just don't like him for some reason."*

As we continue through the examples in this book, this concept of "Liz" scanning everything in our path will be key to understanding how the methods and techniques work.

Emotions:

One more important point: our raw emotions are also stored in "Liz" and directly accessed by the reactionary slots. Micro movements and reactions are almost impossible to control!

The majority of tools provided in this book deal with this primitive non-thinking "Liz" part of our brain. Be aware of your own reactions and thinking to determine how much control your "Liz" has!

Now onto the tools, concepts and ideas that will have you more in control and "Bypassing No."

*Dr. Kevin Hogan refers to "Liz" as the Implicit Mind.

Bypassing 'No' In Business

Chapter 7:
Acknowledging the Gorilla

"All problems become smaller if you don't dodge them but confront them. Touch a thistle timidly and it pricks you; grasp it boldly and its spines crumble."

- William S. Halsey, US Admiral, Pacific, WWII

Carol just took over an existing account, but things have not been going well with the client. Many past issues have been ignored and are festering.

She makes an appointment with the main buyer and asks if their boss can attend, as well as some others involved in servicing the account.

The Meeting:

Tuesday morning Carol meets Jim, the main contact, and they walk to the meeting room where three other people join them.

Jim says, *"This is Carol with BBB and she is here to discuss the services they have been providing."* Carol notes some facial changes in two people (from a smile to a "blank" neutral look) and another participant, Tony, crosses his arms and frowns a bit. She realizes there may be more issues than she first thought.

The Tools:

"It is great to be here, and thank you for taking the time from your busy schedules to meet. I am new to this account and have done an extensive review of the interactions between your organization and ours."

"I realized in my review that not all has been smooth and there have been more than a few issues from your perspective. My sole purpose today is to place each of these issues on the table, determine what might be done to address them, and assure they do not occur in the future."

(Carol is standing with her arms open and her hands with open palms facing upward. This is a very open and safe stance. Open hands let "Liz" see that there is nothing hidden in the hand—very safe. Her very slight smile fits where a broad grin would not be in good taste, and a frown would send the wrong signal. Her eyes are open wide and her eyebrows slightly rise in recognition mode as she looks at each person. ("Liz" is reading safe.)

"I fully realize this may be uncomfortable for you, and disclosing these issues may not be what you desire. Yet, how can we both get better results with these issues in the way?"

(Carol is applying the *Acknowledge the Resistance* or putting the *Gorilla on the Table* method. Most people tend to avoid such issues and try to overcome them by piling up benefits or convincing the other party; "Liz" knows better. Carol has done this twice; once in her opening statement and then by saying: *"this may be uncomfortable."*)

(As Carol views the group, she sees the crossed arms unfold and become positioned in a more relaxed manner in front of them on the table. Tony's frown changes to biting the lower lip, his eyes gazing downwards. Others place their hands on the table as well and lean forward. Two open their notebooks and take out pens. These are all positive changes in Carol's favor.)

Control & Directing:

"Which would be your preference: should I discuss the issues, or would you prefer to present your

view of the situation so we can get the true picture?"

(By providing an option and indicating that the *"true picture"* will unfold when they speak, she has placed a higher value on the words they will say.)

"I'll start first," says Joan. Carol seats herself so she is at the same level as everyone else and pulls out her pad and pen. This is especially important for Carol when dealing with men. To sit in such a manner that she will be at a lower level would put her in a weakened position, and to sit at a level that is actually above that of the others, would run the risk of triggering "Liz," especially in the men. She keeps a neutral and open stance, and she is making good eye contact with a slight neutral smile. "Good eye contact" is best described as making eye contact about 70% of the time, breaking eye contact about 30% of the time. This prevents the "stare down" situation where the other person becomes uneasy and feels overanalyzed.

As Joan unloads her frustrations, Carol encourages her by asking, *"Tell me more about that? Help me understand that better? What did that cause to happen?"* Joan continues to unload showing very aggressive body language, her hands waving at shoulder level and even a clinched fist at one point. When we gesture at, or above the level of our chest, we trigger feelings of excitement in others, feelings that could easily be interpreted as fear or anxiety. To create feelings of trust in others—to find us truthful—gesturing at the level of our naval is most effective.

Carol maintains her open and connected stance. Once Joan is finished, she sighs and the tension in her body disappears. She sits back relaxed and open. Because of what are known as *mirror neurons*, others will start to unconsciously mimic the body language they see as they watch us speak. Since Carol maintained her open and relaxed stance, she was making it easy for Joan to follow her physiologically and ultimately, to say "YES!" (The Gorilla has left the room!)

(By acknowledging the resistance—gorilla—up front and expressing a willingness to talk about it, most resistance disappears. "Liz" goes into neutral mode.)

Success #1:

Carol thanks Joan for her openness and passion for getting results. Joan nods her head and smiles, so do the others except for Tony.

As the others express their views, Carol continues to listen, encourage and maintain her open stance, eye contact, slight smile and open eyes with raised eyebrows. Each goes very well and the issues are all on the table. (More Gorillas have left the room!)

Carol notices that Tony is still tense and somewhat closed in his body stance. He has not made a great deal of eye contact with Carol throughout the meeting. He is the only one that has not expressed his viewpoints.

The Challenge:

"Tony, I wonder if you would be willing to express your thoughts? I'm here to listen and get to the truth with your help."

Tony takes a deep breath, lays his arms and hands alongside his paper, and looks at his pad. He continues this stance as he unloads his frustrations. Carol continues her open stance and eye contact—even though Tony does not—and continues to encourage him to say more. As the rant begins to subside, Tony starts making eye contact with Carol and the others, and his tension begins to subside. As Tony finishes, he sinks back into his chair, arms by his side, sighs and shows a slight smile of relief. *Mirror neurons* to the rescue once again. (The last Gorilla, begrudgingly, leaves the room!)

Carol has pages full of notes. She quickly reviews them and provides everyone with a brief summary of what she feels can be done immediately to address most of the issues. Others will take more effort and Carol asks, *"On these issues, how do you see or feel a cooperative effort might work?"* They all agree on a cooperative effort and that there are internal issues they need to deal with as well. They ask Carol if she could assist them, and she agrees to do so.

(Note the power of the open question versus telling them, or a closed type question. Because it is their idea, they are now committed to the solutions, not just compliant.)

The Big Order:

As the others leave the meeting, they are laughing and smiling. Tony asks Carol to hold up a minute.

"Carol, I greatly appreciate the way you handled this and you have shown me how competent you are. I am in charge of this entire effort, and we have some additional needs for your services. When Jim set this up, my intention was to cancel everything, including your services, but I felt one more chance was in order. Can you come back on Friday morning and discuss the further services we will need?"

What do you think Carol's response was?

Action Review:

How was Carol able to "Bypass No" in this situation?

1. Acknowledged the resistance and the other parties' resistance to deal with it. No Blame!

2. Kept a very open stance and stayed in control of her emotions and body language.
3. Utilized open questions to gain more information once the Gorilla was on the table.
4. Asked for their ideas on how to move forward.

Carol succeeded in being perceived as credible and trustworthy. She was viewed as a partner instead of a salesperson.

Credits to Dr. Eric Knowles and his studies on resistance.

Chapter 8:
Time Machines of the Mind

*Chuck! Chuck! It's Marvin — your cousin, Marvin
BERRY. You know that new sound you're looking for?
Well, listen to this!*

- Back To The Future 1985

I'll let you in on a secret regarding human
behavior, one that you have no doubt experienced
countless times in your life:

> **We are motivated—primarily—by pain and
> pleasure. But, we will work much harder to
> avoid pain than we will to seek pleasure.**

When you know how to use this fact to "Bypass
No," your life will become much easier. Up until now,
however, it's likely that you have been letting this work
against you.

Example:

Suppose I call you one Friday afternoon at 1:30
p.m., *"Hey, some of us are going to fly down to
Albuquerque this weekend to go hot air ballooning and
then do a little exploring in the desert. Wanna' go?"*
You ask, *"When are you leaving?"* *"At 6:30 pm
tonight!"* I reply.

Bypassing 'No' In Business

Predictably, one powerful process has been set in motion. Your mind fills with thoughts of *"I'll have to rush right home, and I don't even think my clothes are washed. I have these checks that I just have to get to the bank, and man, I'll be cutting it close. The kids—I'll have to call their Grandmother and see if she can keep them for the weekend, but she can't get over here to pick them up until about 5:30!"*

If you decide to go, the "pain" you will experience—rushing home, hustling to the bank, washing clothes, calling Grandma, etc. is tonight—NOW! Because the "pain" is lurking so close, you experience a mild, to not-so-mild, fight or flight stress response. Suddenly, you have unconsciously re-prioritized: your #1 goal is to avoid the pain, and one quick way to do this is to say "no" to the trip.

Saying "no" to the trip will be easy. Because your mind is focused on the approaching pain (if you say yes), the benefits of going to Albuquerque haven't even had a chance to make it into your awareness. It is no contest; quickly approaching pain vs. benefits that you don't even get to think about. And the winner is—PAIN!

Let us re-wind and look at it using a different approach. This time, I call you and say, *"Hey, in four months, some of us are going to Albuquerque, New Mexico...blah, blah, blah. Wanna' go?"*

The difference rivals magic. You have four months before you have to think about the pain—the things you will have to do to prepare for the trip. Right NOW, however, you get to bask in the warmth of the good feelings, anticipated experiences, etc., of the trip with your friends. *"YES! Count me in!"* you proclaim.

Getting Yes First:

It is *so* easy to say yes when there is an absence of pain and we have every cell of our body and mind available to enjoy the pleasure we think we might experience by going ahead.

It doesn't end here, though. We tend to be far more confident about what we can do when it involves the future; the farther in the future, the more confident we become about the likelihood that we can do it.

If I ask someone *"If, in six months, I offered you $100,000 dollars to parachute at night, into the ocean, and then swim to the shoreline one-half-mile away, would you do it?"* most people will display a surprising amount of bravado. They will believe they can leap from an airplane into the unforgiving sea below and swim to safety. Change it from *"six months from now"* to *"this Friday,"* however, and you will see their confidence deteriorate.

There are two powerful things at work here. The closer the "pain" is to "now," the less compelling the benefits, and the less confidence we have in ourselves and our abilities. Stated differently, the farther away the "pain," the more compelling the benefits, and the more confidence we have in what we can do. Are you already starting to see how you may have been working against yourself and how you can begin to use this knowledge to make "Bypassing No" much easier from this point forward?

You might be thinking, *"That's all fine, but in my business, I can't be waiting on them to do things in four weeks, months etc. I need to have them do things NOW!"* This works beautifully for NOW situations as well.

Bypassing 'No' In Business

Case Study:

Roger sells home security systems. His leads come via phone calls that people have made after seeing a commercial and then calling a 1-800 number to request information. They have not requested someone to visit them, per se, just some literature in the mail. Roger follows up by calling them and setting an appointment to stop by and discuss the systems they offer.

Roger has dropped by Mr. Smith's office to leave him some materials for review.

"Mr. Smith, before I get going—because I sometimes forget if I don't do it at the start—could I go ahead and schedule a time, three to six months from now, to come back and talk to you in more detail about our security systems?" Mr. Smith is going *"Ahhhhhhhhhh, I can relax; no hard sell coming from this guy."* In most cases, Mr. Smith will be thrilled to go ahead and make the appointment. Once he has, his mind has permission to actually listen, and think about, the true benefits the security system would have for him and his family.

Until the appointment three months in the future had been set, Mr. Smith had the primitive part of his brain on high alert. He would have been in a defensive position, blocking out any possible thoughts of the "pleasure" the security system might offer.

As Roger moves through his presentation, he will notice that he has Mr. Smith's full and relaxed attention. Why wouldn't Mr. Smith pay attention? He has no "pain" to worry about for at least three months!

As the presentation starts winding down, Roger can re-confirm the appointment three months in the future, stating that he will call about a week in advance to remind Mr. Smith. *"Oh, by the way, should this be something that you already know you want to do, I have authorization to issue a 20% discount if you were to do something today."*

If Roger is a good salesperson, he will say this as he is *putting away his material and preparing to leave.* By doing so, he is sending a powerful non-verbal message consistent with his promise of coming back in three months. Meanwhile, Mr. Smith is thinking about the *loss* of his 20% discount if he *lets* Roger get away.

Here is the rub: Roger has to be prepared to leave and to come back three months for the appointment. This is not a lie; Roger has set the appointment and aims to keep it. What has happened, though, is that Mr. Smith has had the opportunity to think about the added sense of security and comfort, and, in one sense already owns the security system. Now, if Roger leaves, he is taking it away and making him pay 20% more when he gives it back in three months. Are you with me?

Key Point:

Push the decision out into the future. Talk about the benefits in the present tense. Then, after you have connected deeply with them, and explained the "pleasures" of your product or service, carefully bring the possibility of a decision *now* back into the mix. Offer, if feasible, some incentive for going ahead *now*. This adds an additional sense of immediate loss or pain, which the customer wants to avoid.

The Body Language of the "Future":

Most people concentrate on the verbal portion of communication. The presenter's body language and non-verbal communication usually goes unnoticed by the "conscious" mind. Simply stated, they will not be aware of body language, but will be impacted by it, nonetheless. When transporting someone's mind into the future, there are several things you can do—non-verbally—to amplify the speed and power with which you do so.

Most people feel the future as being somewhere to the right of them. Conversely, their past will be felt to their left. Why is this important? If I am facing you, your right is on my left. Therefore, if I want to gesture to your future I will be guiding you to my left, which happens to be your right.

Example:

"John, if I were to come back and see you in six months (while gesturing to my left, and John's right) and ask you if you would donate blood for the American Red Cross, what do you think you would say?"

By gesturing to his right, I can take John's mind to the same location it uses when it thinks of any other future event. This really increases John's ability to answer from a position of *"six months from now."*

What else can you do with your body language to increase the reality of the "future"?

Imagine that we are at an amusement park, and you want me to ride a certain ride with you. You will angle your body toward the ride you wanted to go on. You will point your feet in the direction of the ride. When someone is interested in what you have to say, his or her feet will usually be pointing towards you. If not, they will be pointing away from you, or towards the nearest exit. Therefore, use your feet to assist others with getting to the future.

Bypassing 'No' In Business

Some people may experience their "future" and "past" the reverse of most people; they will have the "future" on the left and the "past" on the right. If so, just switch everything to the other side. How do you know which way they think about the past and future? It's as simple as asking them to recall childhood memories and to think about their goals for the future. Then, just notice where they look and gesture in space and time. You will be surprised to find how easy this is to spot, once you know what to look for.

The Language of the "Future:

Now that you know how to use your non-verbal communication to "Bypass No," let's look at how we can make your powers of persuasion even more effective by using language with laser-like precision.

Compare the following sentences:

"Janice, you told me you *are having* some concerns about how this product *would hold* up for you over time; what *are* they?

"Janice, you told me you *have had* some concerns about how this product *will* hold up over time; what were they?"

In the first sentence, when you say, *"Are having,"* you imply that she still is! In the second sentence, *"have had"* moves the concern, ever so slightly to the past. (By the way, you would be gesturing as previously described, to where Janice represents the past—likely her left.)

Then, compare *"would"* in the first sentence to *"will"* in the second. Which one makes you feel more certain about the product holding up? For most people, *"would"* feels like it has a hint of doubt, while "will" feels stronger, thus more likely to happen.

Finally, *"what are they"* in the first sentence implies that she still has the concerns. In the second sentence, *"what were they"* pre-supposes that she no longer has them and is talking about the concerns in a historical, very dissociated point of view.

When I (V.H.) do radio interviews, I am often asked about my reputation for being able to move people beyond their problems in record time, even when years of therapy and other attempts have failed. I often bring up the power of using verb tenses—like those described above—to get them to start moving their problems to the past. I have Richard Bandler and Connirae Andreas to thank for this. I studied hundreds of hours of their recordings to perfect my own use of this incredible linguistic tool.

So, how would you use verb tenses to move someone's thinking and current experience to the future?

Here are some examples

"What if I *were* to come back to you in, let's say, six months ..."

"Imagine what it *would be like* if I *were* to...."

"As you look *into the future* (said while gesturing to their future), what *would* happen if..."

If you combine the use of targeted non-verbal and verbal methods for "Bypassing No," you will soon find yourself more influential than you ever imagined.

Chapter 9:
The Magic of Socrates

"As for me, all I know is that I know nothing."

-Socrates 450 BC

Socrates was smart like a fox and far more insightful. The Greek Philosopher had one goal for students who wanted to discover their "truth." He believed writings by others tainted this discovery, so he used no books or writings in his school!

The Secret:

His main teaching method was the art of questioning. He questioned everything, in every way possible, until there were no more questions available. In this way, a student discovered their own truth about themselves and the world around them.

What does finding your "truth" and questioning have to do with "Bypassing No?" The answer is EVERYTHING!

In virtually every attempt to influence or sell, there is a decision process involved. These decisions can be very simple or very complex based on the situation.

What Socrates understood is by assuming he knew nothing about you, he would then ask highly effective questions to discover who you were, what was important to you and how you perceived things around you.

In this way, he was able to lead you through a decision process that often changed your core beliefs! A very powerful skill when mastered.

The challenge is most of us have somehow been trained to believe that influencing others is all about telling them the benefits and selling them on the idea. In reality, this approach builds up resistance, activates "Liz" into overdrive and pushes others away.

Do you like being told what to do?

Example of Suzie:

Compare Suzie's approach to Dan's.

Suzie works in a furniture store. A married couple, Bill and Dawn, come in to look over bedroom sets.

"Well hi, I'm Suzie and am glad to help you out today, what are you interested in?"

"Possibly a new bedroom set if the quality and price are right," says Dawn.

"Great, the bedroom sets are over here." Suzie leads them to the bedroom displays. *"We have some great units here and great prices too. I'll leave you so you can look around."*

Bill and Dawn look at each other with a puzzled look and shrug their shoulders. They begin to look at all the different displays in a somewhat lost fog.

"Well, have you decided which one you want yet?" Suzie asks as she returns ten minutes later.

"We kind of like this one," says Bill as he points to a very stylish, yet basic, higher-end set.

"Oh wow, that is one of our higher-end units and it's not on sale. It's a really nice set, but if you're

looking for a great price you need to look at this unit over here."

Both Bill and Dawn have slight frowns and even tilt their bodies back in response to Suzie.

"Here are all the great features of this sale unit," says Suzie as she launches into a five-minute dissertation of all the facts and features of the unit on sale.

Bill and Dawn stand with their arms crossed and appear somewhat bored with the situation.

"Well, I think that should settle it. You need to buy this unit; it will save you money and be a great addition to your home."

Bill and Dawn quickly look at each other, Dawn holding back a smirk and Bill rolling his eyes. *"We'll have to think about this for a while,"* was Bill's reply as they left.

Did you feel the resistance and the "no" rising as you viewed Suzie's approach to "telling" them what to buy? This is idiot selling, and buyers are too smart for this.

Example of Dan:

Dan works in a different furniture store and Bill and Dawn decide to check out his store before giving up on buying anything today.

"Good afternoon, I'm Dan and you are?"

"I'm Bill and this is my wife Dawn. We're looking for a good value bedroom set. Where are your displays, and we'll take a look?"

"Most certainly, let me walk you over. By the way, what is causing you to consider a bedroom set at this time?" (Discovering the basis for their decision)

Bypassing 'No' In Business

"Well, ours is 10 years old and rather a cheap unit, we feel it's falling apart and we want a higher-quality unit," Dawn responds.

"If I could ask, how would you describe your style or taste in furniture?" (Has them describing what they want and clarifying it.)

"Hum, how would we?" asked Bill.

Dawn replied, *"I tend to like the older Mission Style with the straight lines and large boards."*

"Sometimes our customers have special needs in their furniture. As you think about this bedroom set, do things like back aches or beds being too high or low or other issues come to mind?" asks Dan. (Not assuming is the mark of a great influencer)

"You know, I don't mind a bed being a bit higher; the lower ones are hard for me to get out of," Bill says smiling.

"Dawn, as you picture the perfect bedroom for your current home, what does it look like?" (Causes them to verify in their mind what they want and take ownership of it.)

"Oh my, it would ....." Dawn replies with animated hands and sparkling, wide eyes.

"Bill, your thoughts?" (Clarifying there is no conflict between their desired outcomes.)

"That makes sense to me; I would like that as well."

"Okay, we're here. I would ask you to stand here and look at this unit from a distance. As you see this unit in your bedroom, how closely does it match your dream picture?" (Causes them to "move in" and verify the picture is correct; they have ownership.)

"Wow, that's a perfect match! Isn't it Bill?" exclaims Dawn with her eyes wide and her mouth open in surprise.

"Absolutely. It's perfect!" says Bill.

Dan steps back and lets them touch, feel and lie on the bedroom set. Bill and Dawn talk about where everything would go and how it would fit for them. (As they touch and feel, ownership is maximized.)

"It's not one of our cheaper-end units. It's a high-quality unit. This will easily last you twenty years. How does this fit your desired value point?" (He is asking them to determine the price/value in their mind.)

"We're not too concerned about the price as long as it has good value and fits our picture of what we want." Bill replies.

"It's Tuesday, what do you feel would have to happen in order for you to experience your new bedroom by this weekend?" (This facultative decision question causing them to deal with the choices needed to meet their objective.)

"Well, if we can take care of the purchase today, can you have it delivered and setup by Saturday?" asks Dawn with anticipation written all over her face.

"This unit is in stock, and we will deliver and set it up Saturday morning if that works for you?"

"Absolutely!" Bill and Dawn say in unison. (Who just bought; or were they sold?)

Application:

The question for you is: did you feel any of the resistance or push back with Dan that you felt with Suzie? Did Dan's questions draw you in as Dawn and Bill were?

Review each of Dan's questions and determine what decisions they caused Bill and Dawn to work through? How did this help Dan to "Bypass No?"

Master this ability and you will "Bypass No" over 90% of the time!

How do you develop this skill and thinking?

Bypassing 'No' In Business

1. First, start, as Socrates did, knowing nothing.
2. Then, be inquisitive and facilitate people's thinking through the choices they have to make.
3. They have sold themselves. That is true influence and "Bypassing No!"

Chapter 10:
The $900 Faucet Lady
Comparative Decision Points

"Our lives are a sum total of the choices we have made."

-Wayne Dyer

Bob is working on a small home project and heads out to buy a new faucet for his kitchen. He heads over to the Faucet Lady to check out prices. *"How can that faucet cost so much?"* Bob asks in utter surprise. *"It's just a faucet for the kitchen sink! The Box Store has one for under $100!"*

Yes, the Box Store does sell similar faucets for under $100. Somehow, the Faucet Lady consistently sells more $900 faucets than she does the $100 faucets that she also carries. The question is how does she do it?

Is it some secret language? Is she so gorgeous that plumbers are dumb-founded? Is this Beverley Hills?

No, this is small-town Midwest, and she is an average 5'2" single mom, working at a plumbing supplier. Yes, most of her customers are plumbers!

The Secret:

The Faucet Lady understands a very simple concept about how we make choices or decisions. She uses this tool to assist plumbers and others in making better, more valuable choices.

Bypassing 'No' In Business

An example:

Say you are moving to St. Louis, MO. You have never lived there before and have no real idea of current property values. You are looking for a home in the $350,000 range, but what that looks like in your current location versus St. Louis can be very different.

For example's sake, you decide a trip to St. Louis is in order. You contact a few realtors and describe what you want in a home.

The first realtor invests a bit of time talking about your needs and desires, then takes you on a tour of twenty homes priced in the $450,000 to $300,000 ranges. After an exhausting thirteen-hour day, you are more confused than ever and still have no real idea of what a good value looks like.

The next day a second realtor meets you and invests an hour grilling you on priorities, life style, likes and dislikes. Her questions really cause you to think and prioritize.

(This is not just for the realtor's benefit; it helps the customer clarify and initiates the decision making process.)

"We are going to look at a very high-end home in the $900,000 range. No, you will not be buying this home. We are looking at it because of the quality and some amenities you would like to see." Upon entering the home, you get the real "WOW" from this one, and the realtor points out what great quality looks like, as well as some unique features. *(This sets a "high" decision reference point and gives a valid reason to view this home.)*

"OK, this next one is a lower-end home that I feel is overpriced. We are looking at it so you understand what to stay away from and what to watch out for." The house is not impressive at all and you

easily see it is not a great value. *(This becomes the "low" decision reference point.)*

The next two homes you visit are dead-on. They feel right, and you know the quality is there. You place an offer on one before noon! *(This one feels right and is a good value: a smart decision point.)*

The difference in the two realtors and their approach to helping you making a decision is the key. We need reference points to make choices. What does a high-quality, well-built home look and feel like? What does a poor-value one look and feel like? With these decision reference points in place, it is much easier to make a good decision faster.

The first realtor provided no comparison of values and did not understand the Law of Contrast.

The Law of Contrast simply states: "When two different objects/ideas are brought closer together, the more obvious the differences become."

Because the second realtor provided three very different reference points (high, low and mid) the comparisons helped you determine "true" value almost immediately and your decision process went faster!

The Faucet Lady:

Back to our $900 Faucet Lady, how did she use this on plumbers and homeowners?

When plumbers came in, she would simply ask *"If you could save time, eliminate call backs and have more profit, would you take 5 minutes to find out how?"* Of course, they would say yes!

"I'll start with this high-end just to give you an idea of what the highest quality looks and feels like." She

hands them the $900 faucet. *"Wow, that is heftier, better quality and this would be an easier installation! But what a price!"*

(Handling an object for as little as ten to thirty seconds instills ownership.)

"This is the $100 unit you generally install; how does it compare?" she asks. *"There is no comparison. It's lighter, cheaply made and a pain to install because of the problems and call backs we get from it,"* the plumber responds.

(Notice who is talking about the differences. When the customer says it, the perceptions become truth.)

"Okay, here are the $300-400 range units, what do you see and feel here?" she asks next. *"This is a good quality unit, with some neat installation features that should save us time and call-backs,"* the plumber tells her.

(Note the type of open questions she is using and who is talking about the product.)

"Which do you feel will give both you and your customer the best value?"

(Her questions are not about the product or price, rather the outcome in terms of value. People buy outcomes on a subconscious level.)

What do you suppose the outcome has been? Yep, most plumbers are buying the $300-500 range and homeowners are buying in the $700-900 range. They carry the $100 units for display only.

Key Points:

To make this work the following points must be initiated in order.

1. The example shown first must be of high quality and be significantly higher—suggest double or

triple—in value than the midrange that is most likely to be purchased.

2. The second example is your low choice reference point so the difference is almost overwhelming.

3. The third reference point is the one that best fits the buyer.

If you are skeptical about how effective this is, closely examine how the big box stores display their TV's. It is from highest to lowest for a reason.

Also, really examine your own decision-making process and see how you determine your final choice. You will find a comparative thought process in action.

Master this and you will be "Bypassing No!"

Dr. Kevin Hogan refers to this as "Flagging."
Dr. Eric Knowles refers to this as "Raising the Comparison."

Bypassing 'No' In Business

Chapter 11:
Overload on Aisle 10!

"Chaos is a name for any order that produces confusion in our minds."

-George Santayana

Today we certainly have choices available to us that were not in existence even a decade ago. At the grocery, I'm Harlan Goerger (H.G.), looking for basic mayonnaise. But where is my regular mayonnaise? There is the shelf full of all kinds of flavors and types. Some are hot, some are mild and some are light. But where is the plain old mayonnaise? After a frustrating five minutes of reviewing the shelf multiple times, I couldn't find it. Guessing they must be out, I figured I'd do without.

It is great that we have so many choices. Product manufacturers are adding more choices every day. The question is, what does this do to our decision making? Does this "Bypass No" or create a situation where there are more "no's?"

Example 1:

Suzan is a sales rep for Brilliant Software and supplies solutions to mid-sized manufacturing companies. She wants to make sure her clients have all the information they need for decision-making. When Suzan makes choices, she always likes to have at least three things to look at.

She has been working with Joe, the President of Creative Structures, for a while now on a new software system for his plant.

Suzan enters Joe's office Tuesday morning and he smiles. *"Good to see you Suzan, I'm looking forward to getting moving on this project. What have you come up with for me?"*

"Here is what I have Joe; this is an important decision for your business so I have several options to go over with you." Joe's smile goes a bit neutral and he gets a somewhat puzzled look on his face.

"Okay, Suzan, show me the first one." Suzan brings out the first option, lays it on Joe's desk, and details why this one could fit. Joe nods his head, has his hands and arms on the desk as he leans forward, and bites his lower lip a bit. (Slight biting of the lower lip indicates some form of tension.) Suzan holds the proposal across the desk from Joe.

"Here is the second one, Joe." Suzan brings out the proposal and again goes over the key points and why this is a good fit. Joe nods his head, as he sits back in his chair. He has his hands on the chair arms, sits erect, and is still biting his lower lip.

"I've saved the best for last, here is the third choice." Once more Suzan goes over the details and reasons why. Joe has pulled away from the desk and pushed his chair slightly back. He frowns as he crosses his arms and stops nodding his head. He is not biting his lower lip, but has a very tight straight lip, and his eyes are not as wide open.

"There we are Joe, our three recommendations that will work for you. Which one do you feel will work best for you?" Joe rocks back and forth in his executive chair, elbows on the chair arms with his fingers open and pressed together in a "steeple" formation. A slight wrinkling of his nose and forehead is barely noticeable.

"Well Suzan, I'll have to have our implementation team take a look at these three to determine what they feel will work. Get back to me on Friday to see which we would go with."

"Well, great Joe, I'll look forward to your answer, and please call me with any questions you or the team may have." Joe nods politely as Suzan leaves the office; he sighs as the door closes and shakes his head in a no fashion and has a frustrated disgusted look on his face.

Example 2:

At two that afternoon, Bill from ManuSoft enters Joe's office. They smile and greet each other. Bill asks, *"Joe can we sit at your table for this, I have some things to show you on the recommendation we have and it would be easier for both of us to view." "Sure Bill, grab a chair."* Bill makes sure he is sitting to Joe's right and somewhat at a right angle to him.

Bill has two copies and gives one to Joe. Because of the position they are seated in, Bill points to key information on Joe's copy and even has Joe check them off as they go. Joe is leaning forward with his arms on the table as he holds the proposal. He is nodding and his eyes are open and bright. This continues as Bill completes his overview of the one-page executive summary.

"Joe, as you review this solution, how do you see it addressing the issues we had discussed?" Bill asks. *"This covers everything we need and will clearly do what we need. I do like the short time frame for starting implementation,"* responds Joe, nodding, and with a slight smile.

"What do you see as the next action needed to get this in place in time for the new product run?" asks Bill while smiling slightly and nodding his head yes.

"Bill, I was ready to go with Brilliant Software," a slight frown of disgust flashes across Joe's face, *"but your solution addresses everything very clearly, even though your proposal of $75,000 is more than their most expensive proposal of $68,000. Let's get started with this. If I sign off today, can your team be in next week to start the installation?"*

"That was our plan; we have two people on standby for your project," replies Bill. *"Great, get them scheduled in with our IT team,"* Joe says with a big nodding yes and a small smile; his body seems void of tension.

Epilogue:

The paperwork has been signed and both Bill and Joe lean back in their chairs and stretch out a bit and seem very at ease. Bill asks, *"If you would Joe, it seemed that Brilliant was the front runner in this decision. What caused that to change, if I may ask?"*

"They are a good company, but they confused me more on this project than I've ever been. I was looking for a solution from someone I trusted. When three options were provided, I got confused and my trust level dropped," replied Joe as he shrugged his shoulders and shook his head no. *"You, on the other hand, had one very good option that clearly addressed what we needed."*

Yes, Suzan did call on Friday and was very confused as to why they lost the sale. I wonder if she was as confused as Joe was the first time she left the office?

Bypassing 'No' In Business

Scientific Studies:

Countless research shows that the more choices a person is given, the greater the chance a "no" decision becomes!

One study shows where a grocery store had 26 samples of jams and jellies out for tasting. Yet, no sales occurred from any of the sampling. Once the store reduced the choices to 16, over 28% of the customers bought a jam or jelly. That is a huge difference for any marketer.

Another study had physicians review a case file. They were asked if they thought it was one particular diagnosis — only one choice. More than 90% agreed that it was. The same file was given to another group of physicians, and they were asked if they felt it was diagnosis "A" or diagnosis "B" — two choices. Some 70% chose one or the other, with the balance making no choice. A third group of physicians was given the same file and provided with three possibilities. The "no" choice and "wanting more testing information" numbers jumped to 78%!

If you want to "Bypass No," you need to limit the number of choices you provide the person you are influencing. Too many choices equal confusion and a "no."

Do as Bill did: understand the person you are influencing and what their real needs (and wants) are. Then provide one choice that fits the bill!

Yes, you will *then* be "Bypassing No!"

Bypassing 'No' In Business

Chapter 12:
Flattery WILL Get You Somewhere!

"There is no effect more disproportionate to its cause than the happiness bestowed by a small compliment."

-Robert Brault

Have you heard the idiom "Flattery will get you nowhere?" It's a catchy phrase, to be sure, but like many popular sayings that have been handed down from one generation to another, it's less than accurate. In fact, in this case, the research shows—and our experience validates—that the opposite is true when you wish to "Bypass No."

Every human being—and I mean *every* human being—favors any action that contributes to a feeling of increased sense of social status. Being acknowledged in a way that makes us feel as though the "price tag" on our worth has gone up, literally floods our brain with chemicals like dopamine, a neurotransmitter that plays a significant role in the brain's reward system.

Being acknowledged can generate good feelings. But, what impact does withholding words of praise, or flattery, have on a person?

How it Works:

Everything we experience is processed by the brain. For example, all physical pain, no matter where in the body it might be experienced, occurs in the brain;

alter what is happening in the brain, and you change the experience someone is having in their leg.

Using FMRI brain imaging equipment, scientists have shown that when someone hears or experiences something that is perceived as a "status lowering" event, the same area of their brain that would light up if they were experiencing back pain would light up as a result of the injurious remark. The little girl that is told, "You're fat!" experiences the comment—neurologically—the same way she would experience skinned up knees; it's painful.

Everyone you meet, from the CEO with $375 shoes, to the janitor with the same trusty $69 boots he has worn to work for the last three years, is craving praise and aching to be noticed in a complimentary way.

Application:

Now, let's talk more specifically about how you can utilize this knowledge and use it to easily "Bypass No."

One of the most common reasons that people feel the need to resist is their lack of self-esteem. They might not know a great deal about life insurance, for example, and therefore, see it in their best interest to be a little bit cautious because they suspect that you know more about life insurance than they do. Therefore, they fear that you could easily take advantage of them. People compensate for their fear and low self-esteem by "bristling up" and demonstrating their power elsewhere.

To the man or woman to whom you have delivered words of sincere praise, you have also delivered a super-charged injection of warmth and vibrancy; they stand a little taller, smile a little brighter, and the twinkle in their eyes becomes obvious.

In short, they feel better about themselves; their self-esteem has increased, and along with it, the sense of increased decision-making skills. When we feel better about ourselves, we are less prone to second guessing our own thoughts, and therefore, the need to resist is tossed out the window.

Example:

Studies have shown that servers can increase their tips by 30% or more, just by kneeling beside the table to take the customer's order. Why? Status and height are inextricably linked. The CEO of a company usually has a high-backed chair, while the chair across from them is diminutive by comparison and sits much lower to the floor. This is not by chance. If you've ever seen the Christmas classic "It's a Wonderful Life," you'll no doubt remember the scene where six-foot-plus Jimmy Stewart walks into "Mr. Potter's" office, and after taking his seat in front of Potter's desk, finds he is just inches from the floor and is forced to look up at the elevated and controlling old miser.

When the wait staff kneels beside the table, they have "elevated" the patron and have literally gotten beneath them. Most people like this—a lot! So much so, that given the opportunity to feel "superior" to the waiter—a form of unconscious praise—they are likely to leave 20% to 30% more for a tip. (Remember "Liz" is always reading the situation and determining safe-fight/flight.)

Does the praise have to be sincere? It should be, but interestingly enough, most people are so hungry for praise and recognition that even if they suspect you are insincere with your praise, it will reduce their resistance significantly. However, why be insincere? I have yet to meet someone that I couldn't find something to compliment them on.

Influence is not about you; it's about the other person. About what you know or observe of them.

Example:

I will never forget the night I stopped for dinner in Knoxville, Tennessee. The woman who arrived to take my order was, without a doubt, the homeliest woman I had ever seen in my life—maybe not the most politically correct way to describe her, but it is certainly the most accurate.

Her gruff and cranky demeanor reflected a life of rejection. She had clearly gotten used to the fact that people did not look at her when they spoke to her.

Determined to look her in the eye when I gave her my order, I raised my head as I said *"I'll have the rib eye, medium-rare, and sour cream with my potato, please"* As I locked my eyes on hers, I stopped; her eyes were the deepest blue I had ever seen. *"I'm sorry; you caught me off guard. I've never seen such intense blue eyes; eyes like that are truly one in a million!"*

I meant it; the only place I had ever seen that particular shade of blue was in the deep ocean waters back in my days in the United States Navy.

Immediately, this woman, who just moments before had me wondering whether I had walked into a restaurant or a morgue, broke into a genuine smile that transformed, not only her physical appearance, but her attitude as well.

To say that I received impeccable service would be an understatement. There is always something you can compliment others on. Find it and "Bypassing No" will become much easier to do.

Case Study:

Mike is a representative for a network marketing company that markets nutritional supplements. He wants to make an appointment with a co-worker, John, who recently commented, "Money is getting tight at our house!" Mike knows that John can be quick to form negative opinions of just about anything and can be very vocal.

Rather than spend hours contemplating how he will overcome John's negativity and brash personality, Mike decides to use praise to reduce—and perhaps eliminate—resistance.

"John, if there is one thing I appreciate about you, it's your ability to look beyond the "bright side" of things that many people get stuck on and accurately examine all aspects of something, to look at not only the good things, but the less than good as well."

"And, you don't pussy foot around and hold back with what you are thinking. I have to tell you how refreshing it is to always know where I stand with you. I'm involved in a new network marketing business, and I know that if anyone is going to be open and honest with me about what they think of it, it's going to be you, John."

One thing you can be sure of when you are watching someone boldly and loudly express their opinion of someone's proposal is that they take pride in their behavior. They often see themselves as the kind of person who will not take guff off anyone and profess, *"I say what's on my mind; if people don't like it, well, that's their problem!"*

The Steps:

Because this is such a powerful tool in "Bypassing No" and setting a positive base to work from, we want to provide a quick formula to help you adopt this as a personal habit.

1. Simply <u>observe</u> one thing about the person, such as *blue eyes.*
2. Ask yourself <u>what this tells you</u> about them or why this stands out. *Bluer than any I have ever seen.*
3. Third, what makes this <u>important to you</u>? *Eyes like that are one in a million.*
4. <u>Tell them</u> the three points you observed!

Body Language of "Flattery":

Here are a few things you can do to make your compliment *even more believable:*

As you prepare to deliver the compliment....**PAUSE**...and count silently to three, before speaking. Silence **COMMANDS** attention, but does so in a way that does *not* trigger resistance. If you've ever been driving along in a daze, listening to a game on the radio, and then, suddenly, the radio goes silent as the station temporarily experiences technical difficulties, then you know how quickly that silence pops you out of your trance.

Example:

"Mike, I noticed something I thought I should tell you... (pause)...the way you handled those people who were upset just a few minutes ago was remarkable. You have a true gift for resolving conflict!"

Next, as you compliment someone, **slightly tilt your head to the side**, exposing one side of your neck. As you do this, the other person's unconscious is thinking: *"Wow, they are so comfortable with what they are saying they are willing to make themselves vulnerable by exposing the extremely vital area of their neck, so they must be telling the truth!"*

When we are lying, or "stressed," we often protect areas of our body that are most vulnerable to attack. The sides of your neck and throat, your stomach, and genitals are areas that you will instinctively protect when you are stressed or fearful. When you leave these areas exposed to "attack," you send a powerful message of *"I'm relaxed and comfortable. I'm telling the truth!"*

Bypassing 'No' In Business

Chapter 13:
Using a "Little Face" to Lower Resistance

"Skepticism has never founded empires, established principals, or changed the world's heart. The great doers in history have always been people of faith."

-Edward Hubbell Chapin

Times have changed dramatically in the last twenty years. Today, a college student is as likely to learn via video conferencing—seated in a classroom watching a monitor, with an instructor 800 miles away—as any other mode of learning. Likewise, salespeople often find themselves presenting by sending a live video stream or perhaps a DVD to a potential client.

Steven Spielberg understands that in any given scene the camera angle can make the difference between an audience that jumps with excitement or nods off to sleep in a darkened theater. Research shows that you need to become your own "Spielberg" when it comes to "Bypassing No."

Times Change:

When Abraham Lincoln was voted President, the nation did not have the opportunity to watch one political analysis after another on television. Today, in the months leading up to an election, people are overloaded with political analysis to the point of nausea.

Bypassing 'No' In Business

Many people would argue that it is the arrogant attitude of a political correspondent that annoys them the most when they are watching someone who supports the opposing political party. Moreover, while this may well be part of the annoyance, new research is showing something else can play a very BIG part.

The Research:

Dianna Mutz, a political scientist at the University of Pennsylvania reveals that, at least in politics, size does matter. When close-ups are shown, giving us a bigger version of the person's head and/or face, it invades (or at least that is how we perceive it) our personal space.

In short, if you are watching someone you are already likely to disagree with, and then the camera zooms in for a close-up making that person's head and face much larger, you will probably find what they have to say as being much less credible.

That's exactly what happened when actors took part in a fake debate with the cameras filming at a middle distance and close-up range. People who watched the debate found the close-up opinions to be less valid and were far more likely to find a grain of truth in those filmed from a mid-range distance.

Application:

How can you use this? If you were going to be producing something viewed by people who may not agree with your message, then you would do well to stay away from the close-up shots and give them a little breathing room by filming from further away.

While the research didn't delve into this application in live settings, my own research and experience confirms that creating more space between yourself and the potentially resistant person—in the beginning—can go a long way in "Bypassing No."

By the way, this also applies to personal space around others. Be aware of your proximity to others and avoid "being in their face."

The Body Language of creating "Little Face" Comfort in person:

When in doubt, move a short distance out. If you determine that someone is comfortable with you at a given distance, you can slowly close the gap. However, if you start out "in their face" and make them uncomfortable in the beginning, you will rattle the cage of "Liz," and once she is awake and nervous, it will be difficult to coax her back to sleep.

There are four different zones, or distances, when it comes to face-to-face communication. These zones are Intimate, Personal, Social and Public.

Intimate Zone: This zone is about 6 inches to 18 inches. We normally reserve this zone for pets, children, family and spouse or significant other. However, once you have established dccp trust with a customer or client, you can access this zone as well. This is a powerful step in "Bypassing No."

Personal Zone: The distance here, is about 18 inches to 48 inches. This zone is utilized for parties and social events.

Social Zone: This zone is about 4 to 12 feet. We feel most comfortable when we keep this distance between us and a stranger, or someone doing work in our home, for example. In short, people we don't yet trust a great deal.

Public Zone: 12 feet and beyond. When we are somewhere where we don't know anyone, or there is a large group of other people, we stay at this distance for maximum comfort.

Keep in mind, if you have set an appointment with someone, you have access to the Social Zone, maybe even the Personal Zone. Closer than that, though, is dangerous territory, and you'll want to make sure they are secure and comfortable with you before you move much closer.

Chapter 14:
Oh No, I've Lost IT!

*"I cannot teach anybody anything;
I can only make them think."*

-Socrates

Have you ever had the feeling that something of value to you is missing? The feeling of dread or loss that comes over you can be devastating. However, it can also motivate you into action to recover what is missing. In influence, this is powerful in getting decisions from others today.

Power of Loss:

To review, we humans tend to avoid pain and move towards pleasure. The pain of loss can cause us to take action now rather than wait.

When applied properly, the sense of loss can close sales and change habits or even beliefs.

In the chapter "The $900 Faucet Lady," we introduced the idea of decision points. This is somewhat similar with a twist.

By creating a future picture of success or gain based on the other person taking an action, we can create ownership of that picture for them. Then, by them not taking action, the success/gain picture goes away and they feel loss. This "pain of loss" is greater than their current comfort and inertia feels. This moves them into taking action now, because they want to move away from the "pain of loss."

The Example:

Jeff is a plant supervisor in charge of thirty people on the floor, as well as three foremen: John, Alex and Bill.

There is a new program to implement on tracking quality, and Jeff is accountable for it going smoothly. He is getting significant push-back from the foremen and crews. This is going to be a big change, with lots of new processes to learn.

Jeff realizes that if he can get the foremen on board he will be more than half way there.

A meeting with the foremen is called. Jeff realizes that telling is not going to work, so he opens with some questions for the foremen to discuss.

Setting it in Motion:

"Guys, I understand you're working hard and you have good people out there, yet I see some frustrations from time to time. I want to help you out if I can. Let's discuss what you are seeing that is frustrating you and the crew." (Jeff is letting them know he understands them; he is like them.)

Bill starts, *"We are really having some schedule issues on the line. It seems we get caught up and just about in control and then we're behind again for some reason."*

John pipes in, *"Yes that does cause us problems, like overtime and additional stress from the sales department when orders are late. Those guys can get demanding."*

"Yes, it does get us frustrated when the line is behind. I just wonder what the real cause is. The crew is working as fast as they can and getting frustrated as well!" Bill adds with a shaking head and arms in the air.

Alex joins the conversation, *"I was looking at some reports last week, and our rework is way up. Last quarter it was not as high, but still it cut our quarter bonus. Is the rework also screwing up our scheduling?"*

All three nod their heads in agreement; perhaps the culprit is being discovered. (The problems are listed by the foremen, not Jeff, so they have discovered them and own them.)

Creating the Ownership:

Jeff asks, *"Let's assume the rework is the culprit here for a moment, what will have to happen to change it on a permanent basis?"* (Facilitative question to uncover choices needed.)

The three look at each other for a moment, then Bill speaks, *"I think we need a different set of processes to flag the rework faster if not immediately. Then we can deal with a small spark instead of a forest fire!"*

Alex nods and slightly smiles, *"Yes, if we can catch the problem earlier, it wouldn't affect the schedule as much, if at all!"*

John adds, *"If we caught the rework right away and the schedules stayed on track, our production numbers would be better, and the quarter bonus should grow as well!"*

Jeff takes over, *"Let me understand what you are saying. If we implemented some type of system to flag the rework problems faster, our outcome would be less stress, schedules being on time, production up and quarterly bonuses up. The crew's morale would be better, and it would be a better place to work. Is this what you see as the outcome?"* (Jeff summarizes and feeds back the picture the foremen have created. This solidifies it and gains a strong agreement from them.)

"Yea!" the foremen agree as they nod yes and smile while glancing at each other.

Jeff has them buying the outcome and taking ownership. (The foremen have determined the outcome and own it.)

The Take Away:

Jeff says, *"Great, that would be wonderful if it could happen. My concern is this: What if we could not implement a system to flag the redo's? What would happen then?"* (Note Jeff takes them back to not taking action and reminds them of the outcome. Thus, he has taken away the positive outcome they have bought into.)

"Oh crap, we would be right back where we started or worse!" Bill retorted.

"I don't even want to think about that! We need to make something happen to get the other outcome," exclaims Alex.

"There is no choice, we have to implement something, even if it takes a lot of effort or change!" spouts John as he shrugs his shoulders in disbelief.

Commitment Time:

"Ok, you guys realize that implementing something like this is going to take time, effort and commitment while still maintaining production numbers. Are you fully committed to it?" asks Jeff. He has his hands open with palms up, raises his eyebrows a bit with a small smile, while nodding yes.

Bill and John lunge forward with a *"We have to, so yes."*

Resistance is Shown:

Alex is nodding his head yes and states, *"But I do have a few questions before I fully commit."*
"What are they Alex?" asks Jeff.
"Who will support us in the implementation and are we going to engineer this system or do you have something in mind?"
"Hey, great questions Alex, as always. How do you feel about either option?" replies Jeff. (Note how Jeff does not respond to the resistance but puts it back in Alex's court.)
"Engineering it ourselves may be interesting, but probably not practical. If we had a turn-key type system that would work, I'd vote for that. Just wondering if the funds are available?" says Alex.

Full Buy In:

"Well here is the good news, corporate has already authorized us to go ahead and implement a system they have pre-approved. They are aware of our challenges and want to help us improve the situation. How do feel about grabbing on while we have the opportunity?" Jeff responds.
"You're kidding us! That's too good to be true; we usually have to fight to get anything," exclaims Bill.
Alex and John are leaning back smiling and shaking their heads in disbelief.
Jeff has them bought in and committed to the new system based on the future outcome, not because the company said so!

"One more thing guys, how are we going to get the crew on board with this?" asks Jeff. (Jeff is cementing the commitment of the foremen by having them problem solve the next step; it is their idea!)

"We have a discussion with them just like we did here. They'll buy in if they see the great outcomes!" says Alex as John and Bill nod in agreement.

"Great, so that's where we will start next week, getting the crew to buy in. In the meantime, consider how we are going to organize to make the time and people available to get the implementation completed as soon as possible," says Jeff.

Actions Review:

1. Note how Jeff got them talking and discovering their problem themselves.
2. Through questioning, he helped them create the future outcome based on a specific action.
3. He took them back to not taking any action and losing the better outcome.
4. He then asked them what they are willing to do, how committed they are.
5. They then strategized the next hurdle.

Yes, this does, and will, work for you if the idea of telling is removed and leading is implemented. You, too, will have your team "Bypassing No!"

Chapter 15:
The Control Factor for Peak Performance

"A man's doubts and fears are his worst enemies."

-William Wrigley Jr.

Many people who have long dreamed of being self-employed or owning their own business allow their desire to simply remain a dream. For each person, the reasons will differ, but at the core for most people is a belief that not having a guaranteed income would be too stressful. Sales *can* be a stressful path to take as a way of putting food on the table. I would argue, though, that it does not have to be more stressful than any other career.

If the last couple of years have highlighted anything worth noticing, it's the fact that no one has a guaranteed income. Sadly, many have discovered that it can all go away in an instant.

Today's Situation:

Today, more than ever, the only real security is found in having the confidence, competence, and ultimately, the willingness to be able to generate income by creating value for others. Whether you have just entered the world of sales and influencing others, or are a seasoned veteran, you will face potentially stressful and frustrating situations.

One critically important piece of the puzzle when it comes to "Bypassing No" is being able to manage your mental and emotional states. Until you have this area of your life under control, the other strategies in this book, as powerful as they are, will fall short of "Bypassing No" as often or as quickly as they could.

One key factor in how much stressing we take part in is how much control we think we have. (By the way, I say "stressing" rather than "stress" to highlight the fact that there is no "stress," but only living human beings engaged in the process of "stressing," or not.) As many self-employed people will tell you (even those experiencing financial hardships), the stress they experience is much less destructive than that of someone with a "guaranteed income and benefits," and for good reason.

> **Key Point: To the degree we feel our control over a situation is limited, our stress response will be more extreme.**

Research:

When researchers were studying the role of control in managing stress, they discovered something far more interesting than what they could have imagined. They had two groups of people they exposed to very loud and irritating noises. Group "A" was given a button and told that by pushing it, they could lessen the frequency and intensity of the noise. In truth, however, the button had no influence whatsoever over the noise. Group "B" had no such button.

Group "A" experienced a significantly lower stress response. As it turns out, it's not our ability to actually control things that matters most; it's the belief that we have control that seems to be the most critical variable.

More Control Issues:

Doctors tell us that exercise is a magnificent stress reducer; in many situations, it IS. This is not always the case, though. In fact, exercise can actually be quite counter-productive. When people are exercising because they *want* to, and actually have some level of *desire* to be doing so, the benefits are incredible. When someone is coerced into exercise, he or she will have an enormous stress response.

Instead of being flooded with a rush of physiological relaxation, their stress hormones will shoot through the ceiling.

I've been self-employed far too long to imagine having to ask someone for a day off or when I can take my lunch break. In fact, I have a phobia—one I'd like to keep forever—and break out in a cold sweat every time I imagine having to wait patiently while someone else gets to decide whether I get to keep my afternoon appointment with my doctor. Studies show I'm not alone.

In terms of cardiovascular risk and metabolic diseases such as diabetes, the formula is rather simple. Those who are in a high expectation/low control position (have a demanding job and exert little control over the process) are hit the hardest.

Between the demand and control variables, demand isn't that significant; those who are in a LOW expectation job, with little control, will be less healthy than those who find themselves in a HIGH demand job, with a great deal of control.

Client Example:

I had a client by the name of D. Johnson when I lived in Guam. He had arrived on the island some ten years before with only $1400 and the desire for something better.

At the time I worked with him, he was easily worth $10 million. From the outside, looking in, the number of things he had going on in his life and the number of times each day he encountered frustration would have looked to be tortuous to the casual observer.

What Johnson experienced, however, and what science proves, is that because he had a high degree of control over his daily behaviors and actions, his body was likely producing far fewer stress hormones than the guy with a fairly low key job, who had to keep his fingers crossed that they would let him take the vacation time he had earned, when HE wanted to take it.

As you consider these findings, it might benefit you to ask:

1. How much control do I currently have in my work?
2. If I choose to stay where I am, what can I do, at the very least, to have the perception of having more control? (Remember, simply believing you have control can make a BIG difference.)
3. How can I give those who work for me a greater feeling of control?
4. What are the consequences to me if I remain in a situation where I feel/have very little control?

Why do so many people continue to be afraid to fly, even though statistics show that it's one of the safest modes of travel around? One word: CONTROL.

When people are buckled into their seat on an airplane, they can feel helpless. There are two to three people in the cockpit, the door is locked, and the passengers are at the mercy of the crew. NO CONTROL.

Conversely, driving a car is statistically one of the most dangerous things we do on any given day. Why don't we tremble when we reach for the door handle? It's simple; we think we can drive better than we actually can, and, because we are behind the wheel—because we feel in CONTROL—we make the mistake of thinking we are safer. When you increase the amount of control you have in your life, or even your perceived amount of control, your stress is reduced.

The Client's Control:

I'll bet you thought this chapter was just about you, but let me ask you something: do you think that the amount of control your client or customer feels they have in a given situation has anything to do with how likely they are to resist, or say "no?" It has *everything* to do with it!

Keep this idea in mind—very close in mind: at the heart of all of the methods you are learning in this book to "Bypass No" is the idea that when people feel they are losing control, they resist and say "no." When they feel like they have more control, they relax, feel good, and are far more likely to say "YES!"

The Body Language of "Relaxed Control":

One of the things I (V.H.) enjoy more than anything else is showing my clients how to inoculate themselves to stress by taking control of their physiology—their body language.

To examine the recipe of body language and non-verbal communication for control, it might be useful to look at its opposite: Frustration. When most people are frustrated, they feel anything but control. In this state of frustration, people have breathing that is shallow and high in their chest. They have their jaw muscles clenched, or at the very least, very tight. Their internal "thinking voice" is very rapid and is in a tense, grating tone of voice, and they typically have tunnel vision; they are only aware of what is directly in front of them, and they have a very narrow field of vision.

As you might have guessed, the physiology of control is very different. When we are experiencing a feeling of relaxed control, we are breathing from low in the stomach, with a much deeper and slower rate of respiration. Our jaw and neck muscles are loose and relaxed. Our thinking voice is slower, and the tonality is pleasant, relaxed, and, well…in control. Finally, our field of vision extends much further into our periphery, and we have what I call "soft eyes."

Remember, because other people are impacted deeply by our body language, and eventually start to shift into whatever it is we are experiencing, we can make it easier for others to experience a state of relaxed control by simply doing it first.

Recipe for Relaxed Control:

- Breath more slowly, from the lower stomach area

- Loosen and relax your jaw and neck muscles
- Slow down your inner voice, and change its tone to one that is more pleasant and relaxed
- Relax your eyes, soften your focus, and become more aware of what is in your peripheral vision

With practice, you will be able to enter this state at will. Your ability to guide others into this state has many rewards.

Chapter 16:
Word Manipulation for Better Information and Increased Focus

"Handle them carefully, for words have more power than atom bombs."

-Pearl Strachan Hurd

Twenty-three years ago, I read my first book on the relationship between linguistic structure (the words we use) and our state of mind; more specifically, how the words we use, allow us, or not, to reach, and then operate from peak performance states.

Perhaps my favorite discovery in this area was what linguists refer to as nominalizations. By definition, a nominalization is the result of taking a process (a verb) and tweaking it a bit, until it sounds like a noun. Sounds fairly innocent, doesn't it? Far from it.

Thing or Idea:

Let's take the word "procrastination," for example. Here's a challenge for you. Pick up a jar, a bucket, any kind of container you wish, and go anywhere you choose to collect enough procrastination to place in your container; even a little bit will be fine. Of course, this sounds silly, and you quickly realize that procrastination is not a thing that can be collected. As a thing, it simply does not exist.

Procrastination is a classic example of turning procrastinating (something you do—a process) into a word that makes the process seem, and more importantly, feel, like a thing you have to get rid of. Since it never existed as a thing in the first place, the goal of "getting rid of procrastination" is ill formed; there's nothing to get rid of, only something to stop DOING.

The Change:

Which seems more likely: getting rid of procrastination or interrupting the act of procrastinating?

Let's look at some other common nominalizations that cause us to fight and struggle against "mind spooks" or perceived "things" that are nothing more than an ever-flowing process:

- *Communication* becomes *communicating*
- *Frustration* becomes *frustrating*
- *Relationship* becomes *relating*
- *Pain* becomes *hurting*
- *Challenge* becomes *challenging*
- *Argument* becomes *arguing*
- *Love* becomes *loving*

See, when we strive to deal with bad communication, we are taking an impossible route. There is only the process of communicating. If, we find that the way we are communicating is not producing the result we like, we can, in an instant, begin communicating in a different manner.

Changing most any process is simple by comparison. I have known people who worked to improve communication challenges for years with no improvement. The real question is what do you find challenging with the way you are communicating?

When you turn the nominalization back into the process from which it was born, you usually feel better immediately.

Tragic Example:

I read an article in the paper this morning about a young woman who was raped. This is tragic. Even more tragic, to me, is that her psychologist suggested a twenty-year treatment plan (I kid you not) to deal with the "trauma" she will "carry."

This well-meaning (I can only hope) psychologist clearly does not understand two critical points: when a patient shows up for help after such an event, they are in a highly suggestible state of mind, and, when an authority figure like a licensed psychologist says, "You'll need treatment for the next twenty years," this quickly becomes reality for the patient, thus, a self-fulfilling prophecy.

This may ruffle some feathers, but there is no such "thing" as "trauma"; there are experiences we find traumatizing, that is, until we no longer do. There are just too many examples in this world of people who have been in traumatizing experiences who have rapid recoveries. Thus, to be comfortable with such nonsense as someone with a supposed education who will tell a young woman that her life will be a wreck without two decades of counseling is intolerable.

I have experienced my fair share of traumatizing experiences in my forty-four years, including, but not limited to, a couple of very near death experiences. They were traumatizing while they were occurring. However, having access to some very innovative methods for processing those events, and, a very deep understanding of human behavior, I didn't have to "carry" any "trauma" about my near death beating. It was over, the moment it was over. Sounds simple, doesn't it? However, far too often, we overlook the obvious.

This young woman will likely experience far more "trauma" from the two decades of keeping these "memories" alive that she did in the sixty minutes of hell over a year ago.

Do I sound peeved? I am; this is an outrageous ignorance of the power of suggesting and our choice of words. Did you catch that? Why did I flag "memories? Because there is no such "thing" as a memory. There is the process of re-membering, and this is a combination of chemical and electrical processes that cause the "memory" to change every time we re-member "it."

Should you attempt to eliminate all nominalizations from your language? Not at all. Nominalizations facilitate the process of freely communicating. However, the next time you are feeling stuck, see if you are describing something as a static event, when in reality, all you need to do is change the process.

The Client Application:

But wait, I've left the best part (or at least as good) for last; you can easily utilize this knowledge of shifting from some static concept to a very fluid and moving process or experience.

You are talking to a potential client or customer, working to discover how your product or service can benefit them the most. He says, *"Well, I'm tired of all of the frustration around here!"* Most sales people will simply nod and say something like *"Oh, yes...I see, that makes sense."* What is wrong with that? They have absolutely no idea what "frustration" means to this person; they know what it means to *them*, but I can assure you, the two are worlds apart.

Since "frustration" is a nominalization, and cannot be found anywhere in the world, we must track it back to the verb it sprang from, and there, we find the process of "frustrating." *"Mr. Jones, what, precisely, do you find frustrating around here?"*

By asking about the process, Mr. Jones will begin giving you information you simply would not have had access to otherwise. Had you moved on from *"Well, I'm tired of all of the frustration around here!"* you would have had the illusion of thinking you know what he was talking about, and he, the illusion of thinking that you knew what he meant, when in fact, you were both wrong. Think "process" and get better information to quickly "Bypass No."

Bypassing 'No' In Business

Chapter 17:
Body Language: "Chin Up's" for "Yes!"

"But behavior in the human being is sometimes a defense, a way of concealing motives and thoughts, as language can be a way of hiding your thoughts and preventing communication."

-Abraham Maslow

Having had the opportunity to travel to, and spend some time in Japan, I have a great deal of respect for the Japanese. In some ways, they show a level of respect for other human beings that is unmatched by any other culture. I put on a pathetic show my first time on snow skis, while vacationing in Japan.

Each time I would wipe out, some kind Japanese man or woman would stop and help me gather up my gear, which was scattered all over the slope. I was informed that this would not have been the case here in the States, and that I would have probably been run over if I had been someplace like Vail, Colorado. I was glad I crashed and burned in Japan!

One thing that is very common in Japan is to greet someone and have them bow to you, as a greeting and show of respect. The deeper they bow, the higher the degree of perceived politeness and respect.

As refreshing as that display of respect can be, it can squash a position of authority here in the United States. More specifically, if you appear to be too passive, you will seem weak and your effectiveness will suffer.

Bypassing 'No' In Business

In the past, I've written a great deal about the many ways you can use head nods, or other similar movements of your head to powerfully communicate and strengthen your verbal message. However, in this article, I am going to address, more precisely, how to nod your head in agreement.

The Nod:

If you stand, keeping your chin parallel to the floor, and then nod your head in agreement, like you are saying "Yes," you may find, like most, that you nod by lowering your chin a few times. If so, don't sweat it, this is how almost everyone does it. Almost.

I have been blessed with the opportunity to meet some of the real power hitters of the business world. Men and women with a great deal of authority and the ability to get people to do things NOW. In watching and studying these people, I noticed a distinct difference in how they nod their head, when compared to how the masses nod.

Would you like to know how? Once again, with your chin parallel to the floor, nod your head in agreement. This time, however, raise your chin a few times. As you do, notice the difference in the strength of your position.

Let me make something very clear: you must make sure the rest of your body language is supporting communication that is effective for the particular context; when you are raising your chin, instead of lowering it, you will run the risk of appearing arrogant unless you are displaying an open and receptive style with the rest of your body. A genuine smile will often do the trick.

Bypassing 'No' In Business

I urge you to nod both ways and notice how one makes you feel passive, while the other empowers you, saying, I agree with you AND I am your equal.

Then, start watching the people around you. You will see a tendency for those in a subservient position nod by moving their chin down, and those in a dominant position, in relation to the person they are talking with, moving their chin up.

As you begin to incorporate this into your daily behavior, you will be taken much more seriously, thus increasing your ability to influence others. Oh, you will also find that others are less likely to attempt to take advantage of you. Not a bad benefit.

Bypassing 'No' In Business

Chapter 18:
Bypassing "No" By Saying "No"

"Our dependency makes slaves out of us, especially if this dependency is a dependency of our self-esteem. If you need encouragement, praise, pats on the back from everybody, then you make everybody your judge."

-Fritz Perls

Nothing stinks as much as "neediness" does to those you wish to influence. I (V.H.) am asked repeatedly, by those in the coaching and consulting business: *"How are you able to get people to pay such big fees for your services?"* My answer is simple: (1) I ask for that much. (2) I try to talk them out of giving it to me.

The typical call between an executive coach and a potential client follows a predictable path; the coach tries to explain or "prove" to the potential client why they are worthy of being hired. They tell them all about what they can do for them, offer to send countless testimonials, and, in short, beg the client to hire them as a coach.

I take a much different approach. First, I am very clear that I do not need anyone's business. I need food, air, water and shelter. I learned this mindset from working with some very wealthy executives many years ago. A mindset that has served me well.

Then, instead of trying to talk them into doing business with me, I turn the tables on them. I say, *"John, as you know, I'm very expensive, can I ask why it is that your situation calls for someone with my ability and skill set? Is it possible that you could get what you are looking for from someone who charges a lot less?"*

Let us look at what has happened in this seemingly simple exchange. First, not only am I not apologizing for my fees, I am spotlighting my fees in such a way that it becomes very clear that I will not negotiate my fee. Then, instead of telling them how I am better than the next coach, I am actually suggesting that they might be happy with another coach and pay much less at the same time. In short, I am putting them in the position of convincing *me* why I should take them on as a client.

> **I am putting them in the position of convincing *me* why I should take them on as a client.**

I cannot begin to tell you how much of a power shift occurs with this strategy. In truth, though, it's not a "strategy"; I'm not willing to negotiate. I have a very simple life and don't have a great deal of overhead. I truly do not "need" the business, and my time with my daughter is my number one priority. I will only work with people I enjoy working with, who will pay me what I ask, or I will do something else, like spend time with my daughter. It's as simple as that. I am willing to say "no" to them.

Instead of telling people, *"I'm the guy for you"* or *"We are the business that is right for you,"* I tell them *"I'm not sure if I'll be a good match for what you need, or, for that matter, if you are the kind of client I would enjoy working with, but I'm willing to find out. If either one of us find that we aren't a good match, we'll call it quits and save each other a lot of time, fair enough?"*

> **Once you are clear on what you really "need" in life, and what you do not, you'll start getting a lot more of what you want out of it.**

Believe me, the first few times you say something like this, you will be quivering on the inside (maybe the outside, too). However, after just a few times you try controlling, rather than defending, not only will it get easier to do, but you'll also feel much better about yourself. No longer will you have to try to convince the world of your worthiness. You will be happy to let people explain why you should allow them to hire you.

Once you are clear on what you really "need" in life, and what you do not, you'll start getting a lot more of what you want out of it.

How to Avoid the Body Language of Appearing "Needy":

- Keep your voice low and deep. When we are stressed and "needy," the pitch and tone of our voice becomes higher and can begin to sound like a whine.
- Keep your shoulders back and your head up. Watch someone who is in the begging mindset, just hoping that someone will give them something. Their shoulders will be rounded and

slumped and they will have their head down a great deal of the time. This is *not* useful for "Bypassing No."

- End your sentences or statements with a downward inflection. Someone who is unsure of themselves and lacking confidence will end their statements with an upward inflection. This makes it sound like a question and undermines your credibility.

The thing I have always appreciated about changing my physiology is how quickly my attitude and mindset will change as well. If you have been behaving in a needy or desperate way, forget about long hours of analyzing why you are this way; shift your body language immediately, and just as immediately, you will find your neediness has vanished, and your position of strength and confidence has grown.

Chapter 19:
Boosting Your Credibility for
Increased Compliance

*"I'm not doing this to be a pop star. I've had plenty of
money and attention. I'm doing it for credibility."*

-Lisa Marie Presley

Few people understand the importance of
credentials; being viewed "THE" expert in their field or
line of work. I have coached many people who had
already achieved a high level of success before we met,
but in almost every case, they had failed miserably at
positioning themselves for easily "Bypassing No" to the
level that they could—and should—have.

One of the first things I ask a new client that has
come to me for coaching is *"What's the name of your
book?"* Most of the time, I hear *"Book? I haven't written
a book..."* This is followed by a firm *"...Yet!"* from me.
Being a published author grants you more credibility, in
the eyes of others, than "M.D." or "Ph.D." after your
name, in most situations. Let me say that again, it's that
profound:

> **Being a published author gives you more
> credibility than "M.D" or "Ph.D" after your
> name.**

Society is full of sayings that hint at the status granted to authors. When we see someone we think is the most knowledgeable person we have ever met on a particular topic, we say things like *"They wrote the book on..."* and we say this, whether they have actually written a book, or not. We just assume that anyone that smart MUST have written one. It works the other way too; we assume that anyone who has written a book MUST be incredibly smart. In our case, that's true (wink, wink).

Here is the rub. If you take the time to do the research in any area, put an outline together, and then fill 150-200 pages with high quality content, you will certainly be an expert in that area. You will know more about the topic than almost anyone. When asked, *"Vince, what makes you a body language expert?"* My answer is, "The fact that I know more about it than almost anyone I encounter, anywhere I go, and can present to an audience for hours, giving them useful information for taking their business to a new level. That's what makes me a body language expert."

Consider this: you might be the most knowledgeable person around when it comes to computers, but chances are good, that unless you are living in "Lone Soul" USA, population three, there are most likely other talented computer "geeks" in your area. Even if you are the best one of the bunch, you won't be seen as a "computer expert"; you will be seen as one of several people who work on computers. Write a book related to computers, and suddenly, you have transcended that group and become an expert. People *will* view you differently, in a very favorable way.

Gone are the days of having to crawl on your belly to publishers, begging them to look at the manuscript you've put your heart and soul into. Self-publishing has become a respected and accepted form of getting your book into print. Ever heard of a little book called *The One Minute Manager* by Ken Blanchard? It was self-published, originally, but was eventually picked up by a bigger publisher.

By the way, many of the big publishers have "scouts" who are continually combing the many self-published books that are written each year. They know that a lot of great stuff isn't even submitted to them anymore. My book, *The Productivity Epiphany,* was originally published by Beckworth Publications, a very small publishing company.

Recently, however, a larger publisher with a far more aggressive marketing budget published it. I am confident they would have never picked it up if I had submitted it directly. However, after it was already in print, they heard good things about it, and they contacted me.

Compare the following: A: John Smith, Life Insurance Agent; B: John Smith, author of "*Intelligent Strategies for Protecting the Future of Your Family*" and Life Insurance Agent. There's no comparison. Having "author of..." has already bypassed countless "no's" that would have needed to be dealt with more overtly.

Think you have to dress well every day to be able to experience tremendous gains using the author strategy? Not a chance. For almost any business you can think of, I can show you countless ways to use a book to blow your credibility sky high. Below are a few examples. (By the way, these don't have to be long books. I have seen many 75 page paperback books do a wonderful job.)

Painting Contractor: *"7 Questions You Must Ask Before You Have Your Home Painted"*

Attorney: *"Winning in the Courtroom"*

Insurance Agent: "How to Deal with High Pressure Sales People and Get the Insurance YOU want"

Therapist: "Secrets of Getting Your Clients/Patients through Their Problems Quickly"

You get the point.

> **The bottom line: Being a published author will put light years ahead of your competitors.**

Let's deal with the faulty, destructive belief of *"I couldn't write a book!"* Could you write a decent paragraph related to your area of expertise? Then, could you write another one? Of course you could. The best way I know to get your book written fast is to start a blog about your topic.

Decide that you are going to write a blog post every day, and then DO IT! You are killing two birds with one stone; the content of your blog post will be the content of your book as well. You may decide to expand on, edit, or otherwise alter your previous blog posts before it goes in your book, but most of the work is already done. By doing a little bit each day, you will be surprised at how quickly you'll be saying, *"Wow, I have enough for a book!"*

All things being equal, the person with the book will "win" nine times out of ten. I have gotten countless speaking engagements because I had published a book and the other speakers had not. Fair? Doesn't matter, that's the way it is. You will either profit from it, or not, but you're not going to change the way the system works regarding credibility and status. The only question is, *"What's the title of YOUR book?"* See you on Amazon soon!

How to get your book written and published:

First, let's look at how you get your book written: YOU WRITE IT! You think I'm kidding? I cannot tell you how many times somebody has asked me *"Could you give me some hints on how to get my book written?"* *"Of course,"* I tell them. *"Write every day, and keep writing each day until it's done!"* Are there strategies that help this process along? Absolutely, but most people tend to overlook the obvious: to write a book, you will have to write a book. It is done one word, one sentence, one paragraph, one page at a time. Just start, and do not stop until you are done. It's really just as simple as that.

For credibility purposes, a book of 110 pages will suffice. A book of about 150-200 pages is what I prefer. Pick your topic. Ask, *"What book title, if one of my potential customers was to pick it up, would give me tons of credibility in their mind?"* If you are already an insurance agent, then you are also an insurance expert; you had to be to get your license. But, until you have published a book, your customers will see you as an insurance "agent" and not, an insurance "expert." The difference between the two is HUGE.

There are several solid publishers out there you can use to self-publish. If this is the route you want to go (and I'd suggest you do), contact me (V.H.) and I can get you on the right path in this area.

It's quite possible to take your book from concept to book-in-hand, for less than $1500. This is one of the best investments for "Bypassing No" you can make.

Just remember, "Author of...." is as good as, and perhaps better than, "M.D." or "Ph.D." for shooting your credibility through the roof.

Bypassing 'No' In Business

Chapter 20:
Turning Your Mind Inside Out to
Make Your Bank Account Go Up

"I like the way Wiseman builds a story in an unconventional way."

-Jim McKay

The most productive salespeople in the world are able to do one thing better than anyone else. They are able to take obstacles and use them as the reasons why they *can* accomplish something. How do they do this? While it's tempting to "blame" it on genetics, the truth is far simpler than that.

Super producers ask a certain kind of question. When a thought like *"I can't sell to that guy, he doesn't like salespeople!"* comes to mind, they immediately use a question that transforms this "dark" thought into a very supportive mentor. They ask, *"How might the fact that he doesn't like salespeople, actually be the reason that I CAN make the sale?"*

They realize that, at least in the immediate future, they cannot change the fact that he has a certain negative attitude about salespeople. They *can*, however, radically shift their perspective, with a well-designed question, and generate possibilities they would never have thought of in a million years

What is a recurring thought in your own life that "tells" you that you cannot do something? Whatever the reason this thought provides as evidence for why you cannot have, do, or be something, use the reason as a pivot point and reverse the question. If, for example, someone says, *"I'd like to go back to school, but I'm a single mother, so I can't,"* ask them, *"How could the fact that you are a single mother actually be the reason why you CAN go back to school?"*

The beauty of this is that you will always get answers to your question. They may not all be workable, but some of them will. If your mind is skilled at making excuses (and it is), you might as well make it search for the kind of excuses that will push you forward.

When you make a statement such as: *"I can't 'X' because of 'Y',"* you have come to a conclusion. Conclusions are the point we reach when we decide to stop thinking. Questions, on the other hand, invite your mind to start generating ideas. Questions like: *"How could 'X' really be the reason why I can be, do, or have 'Y'?"* will open the flood gates to insights, ideas and strategies that will take us from point A to point B in record time.

Limitations aren't "out there" as much as we would like to believe. Most of the limitations that we face are generated within us, *about* "out there."

We can use the *"How could 'X' be the reason why I CAN 'Y'?"* formula to re-orient ourselves, from the inside out—and this is always where we should start. We can also use this formula to re-orient someone else's thinking, too.

When someone says: *"I'd love to buy life insurance from you, but I just got laid off from my job."* Instead of coming back with the classic, *"That's exactly why you HAVE to buy life insurance, do you really want to put your family through the stress of, blah, blah, blah...,"* you could use the formula and say, *"I'm curious, how might the fact that you just got laid off, actually be the reason that you can buy life insurance?"*

In print, this may seem absurd. However, when you are congruent, and ask this question from a relaxed place of deep curiosity, you'll be surprised at how many intelligent answers people will come up with. Moreover, the fact that *they* come up with their answer is what makes this work so well.

Real Client Story:

Here is an example from a client session I had recently:

Client: *"I need to create some multi-media products to offer at my conferences, but there are so many people already selling them, I'm afraid the market might be saturated."*

Vince: *"How might the fact that there are already so many people selling them, actually be the reason that you should go ahead and create the multi-media products?"* (I have no idea what the answer to this question will be and have no predetermined direction in which I am trying to take him.)

Client: (after a long pause) *"Hmmm, well, I guess the fact that there are already so many, and that they are pretty much all the same thing packaged differently, means that the market is probably yearning for something fresh, and truly new!"*

What is important to remember here, is that my client probably would not have thought of this unless the *"How could 'X' be the reason why I can 'Y'?"* formula was applied. Our minds, once in a rut, tend to stay there, and a question like this is one of the best "rut-busters" I have ever witnessed.

As far as body language and non-verbal communication are concerned when you ask these questions, lower your voice, tilt your head slightly, and become as curious as you possibly can about what their answer will be. This will powerfully communicate that you are not being sarcastic and are sincerely interested in what the answer is. When you congruently act as though there will be an answer, they will usually be able to generate one. And, the answer they generate will be ten times better than one you supply!

The Body Language of "Inside Out":

When you ask: *"How could X really be the reason why you need to/should/can/might Y?"* it is critically important that you have all of your non-verbal communication lined up just right. If not, you will come off sounding sarcastic.

Ask the question with such an intense sense of curiosity and confidence that they do a deep inner search and come up with an answer that makes perfect sense to them. You are *curious* because you don't know what the answer will be, but you are equally *confident,* because you trust that they do.

> **It's amazing how much others believe in themselves when they can see that we believe in them.**

After you have asked the question, they might look at you as if confused. If they see any doubt in your body language, they will stay confused. However, if they see a confident look of expectancy in you, then suddenly, it will become meaningful and thus possible, in their mind. In other words, whether they come up with a good answer—or for that matter, an answer at all—depends upon how congruent you are with your body language.

Bypassing 'No' In Business

First, after you ask the question, make direct eye contact that signals: *"I have all night, and I'll wait patiently until you find the answer, because I know it's in there."* It is important that you say *nothing*. Just continue making eye contact. After about ten seconds, slowly, almost imperceptivity, start nodding your head yes. This will signal that you have complete faith that they have an answer. The moment they start to say *anything*, softly smile and nod your head a little more overtly, as if they are on the cusp of a big breakthrough.

It's amazing how much others believe in themselves when they can see that we believe in them.

Bypassing 'No' In Business

Chapter 21:
Which Way is Your Goose Flying?

Our ability to influence ourselves and others to action is a critical factor in getting things done. You are either going to do something yourself or delegate the task to someone else. Are there any tasks you've decided to take on that you still haven't completed?

Have you delegated some project and been frustrated because someone is dragging their feet? I am guessing you were able to answer "yes" to both questions.

Your ability to influence others will soar the moment you understand the concept I'm about to reveal. First, I want to share something with you:

Flying Geese:

I am sure you already know that geese fly south for the winter. (This, by the way, is a pretty good idea—many people have caught on to this.) In the spring, they'll make a return trip north.

If I want to influence a goose, I need to know in what direction he's already going. By placing mounds of grain in various places, I can get a goose that is flying south to deviate from his course, as long as it allows him to continue in a southerly direction. I can influence the goose to fly southeast, or southwest. In either case, the goose is still going in the direction it has been biologically programmed to go.

If a goose is flying south for the winter, and I want to influence the goose to go north, it will be difficult, at best. Even if I get this goose to go north, it will be short-term. Eventually, the pull to go south will be overwhelming, and it will begin heading south again.

What's the one concept that will amplify your ability to influence?

> A goal of persuading *anyone,* and *everyone,* to buy what you are selling will lead to problems.

Fighting the Natural Tendencies:

If I am selling fishing poles, I don't want to sell one to someone who doesn't fish. They will only regret the purchase later and unconsciously resent me for talking them into buying something they really didn't want. If I want to sell a truckload of fishing poles, I need to find a truckload of people who are crazy about fishing. Obvious? It should be; but, it's not.

If you are an entrepreneur, looking for someone to finance a new internet-based promotional campaign, finding an investor who is already "flying south" would make this a much more enjoyable process. Someone that has the money to back you and has already experienced the effectiveness of well-planned internet marketing is already "flying south." An older investor with very little knowledge or experience with internet-based marketing is "flying north"—no matter how much money they have to invest.

Talk to a room full of investors "flying south," and you'll have the needed financing. Talk to a room full of investors "flying north," and you might get the help you need—you might, but it will be like pulling teeth, and the lack of conviction on the part of the investor will eventually take its toll on you as well.

Bypassing 'No' In Business

Beliefs play a big role in determining what direction someone is flying. Take for example: *"But Vince, I sell air filters, and everyone needs cleaner air!"*

While everyone may benefit from breathing cleaner air, those that believe: *"The air I breathe is clean enough already; a little dirty air never hurt anyone,"* are "flying north."

A customer that believes: *"Our air is so filthy, it's a wonder I'm not already dead,"* will quickly identify, and agree, with the importance of an air filter. This is the "goose headed south" I was looking for.

Is your marketing set up to attract "geese going your direction," or, are you just trying to attract "geese"?

When you market in a way that will filter out the "geese" going the opposite direction, you'll find more joy in what you do, have more energy at the end of the day, and "Bypass No!"

Bypassing 'No' In Business

Chapter 22:
Why Having Goals Can Undermine Your Ability to Influence and Produce

"Not brute force but only persuasion and faith are the kings of this world."

-Thomas Carlyle

Does it shock you to hear that having goals can destroy your life? If so, please know that your thinking is normal. After all, we've heard one speaker after another talk about the virtues of having a goal, and how we can achieve anything we want if we'll just set goals.

I'll bet you've even heard about the study on goals conducted at Yale during years where they surveyed graduating seniors and found that only 3% of them had clear and specific written goals. Twenty years later, they surveyed these same seniors and found that the 3% with written goals had accumulated more wealth than the other 97% combined.

Another Myth:

Impressive, right? The story is impressive; but you see, there's one BIG problem with the story: it's a myth. Yale University Research Associate, Beverly Waters completed an extensive search, digging through archives and found that the study is an urban myth—it NEVER HAPPENED.

On my own personal development path, I bought into this myth as well. So did just about everyone else that was striving to improve his or her life.

Let me make one thing clear: Goals ARE powerful tools for accomplishing more than you would have without them, but only if you are able to avoid the mistake that we'll get to in a moment.

The Reality:

First, though, take a moment to consider all of the things in your life that you have accomplished, things you are proud of, that you didn't set a goal for. Most likely, some of your greatest accomplishments did not come from a written goal—you just did what had to be done.

Next (and this can be a little depressing), think of all the things you set goals for, but never achieved. If you have been a "goal setter" for many years, don't think about this for too long, because this list might be longer than you'd like.

I remember a day in February 1986, when I received my license as an insurance agent in the State of Missouri. What I could not have known at the time, was that my internal state was about to become a "state of misery."

I decided to sell insurance after I saw the amount of money my friends were making. They were buying new cars, wearing new suits, and cashing checks for a week that were bigger than what I was making all month. I had a burning desire to have that kind of income in the near future.

There were two major problems with that goal. First, it focused on income. Second, I was thinking only of the future. In a moment, you'll see just how these two slip-ups are responsible for feelings of depression in millions of people each year.

Most people, when establishing their goal, focus on how they will feel (how happy, how rich, how content, how ecstatic—you name it) *after* they have accomplished their goal. They rationalize: *"If I pick something very rewarding, I'll be able to endure anything to get there."*

Almost everyone is overly optimistic about their ability to do things in the future. What they forget about, however, is that the future is only a concept, a thought, and that the only thing that ever truly exists is NOW. Life is one present moment after the other from cradle to grave.

The Secret of Goals:

If the goal you pick is one that will not allow you to feel inspired, driven, excited, and invigorated in every present moment between now and the achievement of your goal, then you have picked the wrong goal.

If you are about to write down a goal, ask, *"How will having this goal impact my 'right now's'?"* *"Will this help me to wake up and feel excited to jump out of bed and get started?"* *"Will having this goal cause me to have to pry myself away from it each night to go to bed?"* If the answer is, *"Yes!"* press on. If the answer is *"No!"* move on.

I will never forget the day that I realized what a bunch of malarkey "affirmations" were. Oh, believe me, I've done my fair share, and I have discovered a rare situation where they are perhaps beneficial, but in almost every arena that affirmations are promoted, they are not only an utter and complete waste of time, they indicate something far more serious.

Another Myth:

If you have to use affirmations to get yourself to do the things necessary to accomplish your goal, scrap that goal, and go back to the drawing board. Do you think that Edison had to do affirmations to spend twenty hours a day in his lab? Do you think the Wright brothers did affirmations to be pumped up so they could work on their "flying machine?" Do you think Bill Gates was doing affirmations when he ditched college to pursue his work with computers? Absolutely not!

It's not my "goal" to write every day. I do not do affirmations that say, "I like to write, I like to write, I like to write…" I write because some years ago, I finally connected with my core drives in life. Once I did this, it all became rather effortless by comparison.

Writing, speaking, teaching, training and coaching (all things that enrich the lives of others), are things I excel at doing. Things I am passionate about. Therefore, they are what I do. It's really just as simple as that. To the degree that you need to use willpower, affirmations and "rah, rah" motivation to continue what you are doing, you are out of alignment with your purpose.

If what I am saying were true, then why would we even want to set goals? That is a good question, and fortunately, there is a good answer.

Some of my current goals are to write at least ten more books, create twenty more audio programs and live a few days with tribesmen in the Amazon. I do not need affirmations.

I have to write every day. I feel compelled to share my ideas with others. The only reason I write down a goal is to help me map out my "how's" and to stay on course. If a desire is not already burning within me, I do not bother calling it a goal. If I did, I would never harness enough motivation to take action.

I remember sitting next to a gentleman on an airplane once who was known for turning struggling companies into booming businesses. I asked him, *"How do you motivate your people?"* He replied, *"I don't; I just hire motivated people!"* He knew the secret I had just recently discovered. He just figured it out a long time before I did.

The Formula:

Here's a simple formula for determining whether a goal is one you should keep or dump NOW:

> **Whatever your goal is, notice how it makes you feel right NOW about the things you'll have to do in the future to achieve that goal.**

For example, if you want to become a physician, forget about how you'll feel after you're a doctor. That's irrelevant. The only thing you should be concerned with is how you feel when you think about NOW, and how you will feel in all of those "now's" that will have to take place before you are a doctor.

If sitting in the classes that you'll need to take won't feel as exciting to you as the thought of being a doctor, run the other way as fast as you can; I don't want you to be a doctor. You might wind up like tens of thousands of other doctors who, after having started their practice, find that they really picked the wrong career. I don't want that doctor operating on me!

The doctor I want to deal with is the one who enjoyed becoming a doctor every step of the way; the one who couldn't wait to get to class each day. Are there doctors like this? Yes. I worked in a hospital environment for five years and met several. Sadly, I have met far more that are only doctors now because they were chasing the dream instead of asking, *"How does this goal make me feel NOW?"* from the very beginning.

Forget about what other people think you should do. Forget about what society or your culture says you should do. There is only one path that you should take; the one you want to walk on.

When you take this path, you stand the greatest chance of contributing to others in a significant way. In addition, remember, we can only be successful to the degree that we are delivering value to others. The more value we deliver, and the more people we deliver it to, the more successful we become.

How This Bypasses No:

Why would I bring this up in a book on "Bypassing No" and influencing others? I cannot tell you how many people I've met who were in a profession they detested, or were trying to sell a product or service they had no passion for.

When this is the case, you can utilize the strategies for "Bypassing No," but when you hear "yes" from a customer, it will most likely be from someone who would have said "yes" anyway.

There are few things as important in influencing others as a deep belief in what you wish them to do. With that passion, the world is yours, and the methods in this book will do wonders. Without it, well...let's just say it won't be pretty.

If you already have that passion about what you do, that's great. If you don't, consider putting this book down, writing your resignation, and finding something that excites you the moment you open your eyes in the morning.

This life is a one shot deal, as far as I can tell. Make it one worth talking about.

Bypassing 'No' In Business

Chapter 23:
Conversations with a Ghost

"Any problem, big or small, within a family, always seems to start with bad communication. Someone isn't listening."

-Emma Thompson

When I tell people that I've used my cell phone countless times to get my suggestion under a client's analytical radar, effortlessly "Bypassing No," they look at me a little strange. *"What do you mean? How do you use a cell phone to do that?"* they ask with a quizzical look.

I (V.H.) felt this book was one that I was destined to write; I am your classic "polarity responder," when I feel like someone is pushing me, I push back— only harder. I have been that way as long as my mother can remember. The more intense the stressors, the more likely I am to push back. As an adult, I have learned innovative strategies to re-direct my mind, thus, my behaviors, but they don't always come to mind in a given situation.

You will run into many people like this in life. They can be the sweetest, kindest and most cooperative people you will ever meet. I am the kind of guy who doesn't bother sending back a steak not cooked as I wanted; I just let it slide. Tell me what I "need" to do while using an aggressive, cocky, authoritative, "all knowing" tone of voice, and you'll see a different side of me, though. I am not alone. The question you might ask yourself is, *"Do I have an effective strategy for working with, and influencing, people like this?"* If not, you're missing out.

I have discussed this at length with several other social scientists. While there is no conclusive evidence, many of us are convinced that there is a strong genetic component to this.

My daughter has demonstrated many of the same responses since she was a toddler. I have diligently worked to teach her strategies to manage her feelings and occasional desire to "rebel." I know the turmoil it caused for me early on in life.

Depending on my daughter's mood, how well rested she is, and how long it's been since she's eaten, she may, or may not, respond too well to the suggestion that *"The best athletes are the ones that hustle on and off of the field!"* However...

Maybe you've noticed the tendency for people to eavesdrop on conversations going on nearby. Sometimes, the more you are not supposed to hear the conversation, the more you want to. Why not use this fact of human nature to your benefit?

So if I want my daughter to embrace the idea that *"The best athletes are the ones that hustle on and off of the field,"* I will engage in a mock conversation and say (into the phone), *"The best athletes are the ones that hustle on and off of the field!"* There is no reason for her to resist the message. It's not even "intended" for her.

I have used this with clients repeatedly over the years with great success. I time it so that I'm "on the phone" when my client arrives. I will motion for them to have a seat and let them know that I'll be with them in a minute. Then, knowing they are listening, I deliver the suggestion via my cell phone.

Occasionally, when I teach this method, someone will say *"I'm not sure how ethical that is. I mean, isn't that lying?"* I ask, *"Do you have kids or nieces/nephews?"* *"Yes"* is the most frequent reply. *"Good, because this is no less unethical than you telling them that a fat guy in a red suit comes down the chimney, or that a big rabbit leaves eggs, or a fairy collects their teeth and leaves them money!"*

If your intentions are evil, then your method, whatever it may be, will be just as evil. If your intentions are beneficial, then you shouldn't get anymore hung up on using the phone technique than you do about telling someone you like their new sweater, when in fact, you think it's hideous.

Here is an example:

Your client comes in for their appointment to discuss life insurance. You, of course, are "on the phone." The suggestion you want them to embrace is that life insurance is the single most important decision most adults will ever make.

When they come in, you say into the phone, *"Mike, most people don't grasp the importance of that concept. The fact that you know that life insurance is the single most important decision most adults will ever make demonstrates your financial intelligence."*

In truth, life insurance IS that important. You are trying to ensure that your client's tendency to resist does not get in the way of him accepting this important fact.

The Body Language of Talking to a "Ghost":

It seems simple, but it's not as easy as you think. Carrying on a one-sided conversation can make you feel like a low "B" grade actor until you practice it a few times.

While you are on the phone, actually talking to someone else, stand in front of a mirror so you can see your individual style. Pay attention to how you hold the phone, the gestures you use, and your facial expressions. This will give you a blueprint to work from and allow you to compare your "ghost" calls with the real ones.

I prefer to sit at an angle, showing only my profile to the person whom my message is intended for. If my client is a very skeptical type, then just before I deliver the suggestion that is critical for my client to hear, I actually turn *away* from them. This has the effect of further demonstrating that the message is "private" and only for the person on the other end of the phone. I do this to create an added buffer, going even one step further to make sure that my message is accepted and heard by my client, without triggering any internal resistance.

If my client is less skeptical, I will turn from my profile view, and *look right at them* when I deliver the suggestion to the "ghost."

I wish you great success with your "ghostly" experiences.

Chapter 24:
The News Anchor's Secret

"Curiosity is as much the parent of attention, as attention is of memory."

-Richard Whately

Imagine that you are watching the news, and you hear the anchor say, *"There is new information out tonight about a product found in almost every home in America that's slowly killing you and your family. Can you guess what it is? We'll tell you, when we come back. Now, we go to a commercial."* Are you going to turn off the television after hearing that?

News agencies know that if they don't hook you, you will probably get up and do something else when they go to the commercial. And, after all, commercials pay the rent!

Most news anchors don't really think about the psychology behind this; they are simply reading the teleprompter—written by folks who DO understand.

We have a strong desire for closure. For decades, the "Soaps" have been watched faithfully, day after day. They even have magazines dedicated to these shows to give watchers even more information. Not only do the "Soaps" leave you hanging at the end of the show, but they also keep the tension going during the show by jumping from one sub-plot to the next. They break off from each one just as it was about to reach a climactic end, but just before it does, they run another story line.

By the time the "Soap" has ended that day, the viewer's brain was chemically altered. They were "programmed" to keep thinking (both consciously and unconsciously) about the show, and are so curious about what will happen next, that they actually schedule the following day's activities around the show time. That, my friend, is a powerful and elegant way to "Bypass No!"

So, let's get down to the nitty gritty and talk about how YOU can use this method to "Bypass No." It's quite simple, actually. First, you have to be able to captivate the person you are dealing with by using a story or something of interest to them. It will not be effective if you cannot do that.

Now, I am going to discuss a non-verbal method you can use to captivate and entrance others, whether that is one person or a group of one-thousand.

> **"A whisper is like salt and pepper. A little makes bland food tasty; too much makes bland food inedible!"**

This is something that very few people ever understand. Yet, for those who do, it is to communication what the light saber is to a Jedi. Most people try to capture someone's attention by speaking louder; they raise their voice almost to the point of shouting. But, if you want to narrow someone's focus you will accomplish more by lowering your voice to a whisper. If I raise my voice, it requires you to focus *less* than you had been. If I lower my voice to a whisper, you have to "lean into it"; you have to zero in with the focus of a bomb technician.

When I talk about the use of the whisper in workshops, I say, *"A whisper is like salt and pepper. A little makes bland food tasty; too much makes bland food inedible!"* If you over use the whisper technique it will lose its effectiveness. Used sparingly, it is one of the best tools for intensifying attention I have ever seen.

The formula for using the "News Anchor's Secret" is: **Have you heard about_____? It's amazing, but before I tell you, I want to ask you a question_____. Okay, I was telling you about_____, well here it is_____.**

Here is what it might look like when used by a life insurance agent:

"Have you heard the new discovery about the one thing that will take years off your life? It's quite amazing, really, but first let me ask you a question: <u>taking the $500,000 Term Life Policy we've discussed is intelligent, and is the best choice for your situation</u>; do you know how many people wait too late, and wind up with poor health, unable to get insurance? Okay, anyway, the thing that everyone does, but yet, is trimming years off people lives—unnecessarily: people who chronically get too little sleep run a greater risk of developing diabetes and heart disease, taking years off their life. Such an easy thing to remedy, don't you think?"

Let me break this down piece by piece. First, you have created a "cliff hanger" by asking a question related to them personally. Then you say, *"First, I want to ask you a question…"* Once again, you have amplified their attention. When we know we will be asked a question, we listen closely, so we will understand the question and have the best chance of being able to answer. You have heightened their focus twice.

Next, and this is a BIG one, you follow up with the statement or suggestion that you want them to accept—you "Bypass No." While they are in "open" mode, you deliver the suggestion: *"Taking the $500,000 Term Life Policy we've discussed is intelligent, and is the best choice for your situation."* Then immediately follow up with the question of *"Do you know how many people wait too late, and wind up with poor health, unable to get insurance?"* This satisfies the part of their mind that was waiting for a question.

Finally, you wrap things up by closing the loop. *"Okay, anyway, the thing that everyone does, but yet, is trimming years off peoples' lives, unnecessarily. People who chronically get too little sleep run a greater risk of developing diabetes and heart disease, taking years off their life. Such an easy thing to remedy, don't you think?"*

You can open with a story. Radio Icon, Paul Harvey was a master at this with his "the rest of the story" broadcasts. If you haven't heard any of them, I would urge you to find a copy and listen to them repeatedly. Not only will you find them enjoyable, but you will also be learning from one of the best teachers out there about how to capture the interest of your audience. Paul Harvey would cut off from his story, after having taken your curiosity to Mt. Everest heights, and break to a commercial. Smart! When they came back, you heard "the rest of the story."

Chapter 25:
Have You Heard About...?

*"Anyone who has obeyed nature by transmitting a piece
of gossip experiences the explosive relief that
accompanies the satisfying of a primary need."*

-Primo Levi

During the brief time I sold insurance some twenty-five years ago, I remember being told, *"Never allow them to set a follow-up appointment; close right THEN!"* The rationale was that all they were trying to do was get you out of the house, and if you left, you would never get back in. In many cases, that was true. But, with a little effort pre-qualifying them, it would have been easy to figure out which ones they were.

Some people might make two to four follow-up appointments before they purchase your product or service. If you are selling Lear Jets, we are talking several million dollars. If someone wants to think about it, or see about financing etc., then I would not suggest pulling out your legal pad and doing the "Ben Franklin" close.

When someone you have already qualified says *"Let's get together next Tuesday afternoon; I want to talk to my partners"* and you do the "Ben Franklin" close—or any close for that matter—what you're really doing is creating pressure that will likely be resisted. Ultimately, it could culminate with the loss of the sale altogether.

Once you have made a future appointment, the last thing you want is for all your groundwork to have been a waste of time. There are certain things you should "stick" in their mind like super glue. Fortunately, there are several very good ways of doing just that.

Benjamin Franklin said, *"Three people can keep a secret—if two of them are dead!"* He was right. I chuckle each time I hear someone say, *"I don't like to gossip, but..."* The fact is, we do like to gossip. Simply saying, *"I probably shouldn't tell you this, but..."* makes virtually anything you say more memorable.

Alex Mesoudi and Andrew Whiten of the University of St. Andrews teamed up with Robin Dunbar from the University of Liverpool to find out more about how gossip spreads; more specifically, whether it goes through groups faster and more effectively than non-gossip information.

The results were staggering. They found that information that was "gossip-like" was more easily remembered, with recall of far more details, than non-gossip information.

Does this mean you have to go around spreading rumors to get people to remember something? Of course not, and, in fact, I would suggest that you don't. It's only important that it has the feel of gossip. This is easily accomplished by saying, *"I probably shouldn't tell you this, but..."* Does it make sense? Not really. But it does make a BIG difference!

"I probably shouldn't tell you this, but this sofa just came in last week, and this model is one that everyone tells us they just love!" You're thinking, *"That sounds weird, won't they think so, too?"* In short, no. Everything in this book was tested in countless situations and has received tons of feedback on its effectiveness.

What *will* happen, when you use this method, is that the person will remember the conversation longer and will recall it with more detail. This is exactly what you want. If they happen to say, *"Why shouldn't you tell me that?"* just chuckle and say, *"Because I didn't want you to think I was trying to sell you something!"*

Anytime I have ever done this, they laugh too, and what I said has become even more memorable, because the humor has marked it even more clearly. Most of the time, they won't say a word about it. If you want to give yourself a buffer, though, just tag a question on to the end. *"I probably shouldn't tell you this, but this sofa just came in last week, and this model is one that everyone tells us they just love! Have you seen one like this in someone's home, or just here in the store?"*

By sticking the question on the end, you will take their mind away from the *"I probably shouldn't tell you this..."* part, and by the time they process and answer your question, any "weirdness" will have long ago dissolved.

Before using this technique, think up a few key ideas that you want them to have "stuck" in their mind until you meet again. Then, simply place your comments inside the *"I probably shouldn't tell you this..."* format. Be prepared for them to recall your suggestions the next time you see them—to collect the check.

The Body Language of "Have you heard about…?":

To congruently engage in the "Have you heard about…" method, you will want to do a couple of key things with non-verbal communication. When you ask the *"Have you heard about…."* question, lower your voice (as though no one else should hear the "scoop"), and inject your voice with a sense of excitement, as if you have one of the best-kept secrets around. The combination of lowering your voice and sounding excited will narrow their attention and mark your message as one that is truly worth hearing. Also, lean in a little closer to the other person as you speak.

Bypassing 'No' In Business

If you think about it, these are all things you do when you really are gossiping with someone. I know *you* do not gossip, but it is what other people do. You want your non-verbal behavior lined up with the content of your message. If you can do this, you will "Bypass No" with ease.

Chapter 26:
I Hear Voices

"As a singer I tried on all these hats, these voices, these clothes, and eventually out came me."

-Carly Simon

The area of your brain that processes sound (auditory cortex), and the area that processes feelings (kinesthetic cortex), have a considerable amount of overlap. Sounds and feelings are often the same. Have you ever heard someone drag his or her fingernails down a chalkboard? (I am betting you just made some kind of physical movement—just from reading that!) The fact is, sound influences us in surprisingly profound ways.

The most important sound you will likely project to others is your own voice. How you use your voice can mean the difference between "Bypassing No" and running into a solid wall of "no." A low-pitched voice is a more influential voice; people extend more trust to, and feel more secure around, someone that has a low-pitched voice. I have seen salespeople radically increase their income just by shifting their voice to a lower range. Our unconscious mind is soothed by a low-speaking voice.

"But I don't have a deep voice—not even close!" No matter where your voice is now, it is simple to make shifts that allow you to use your voice to impact others deeply. Where you breathe from makes a big difference. Breathing from high in your chest will produce a higher-pitched, even nasal sounding voice. When you breathe from your stomach area, your voice will be deeper and

more resonant. Remember, a lower pitched voice is one perceived as being more credible. Simply put your hand on your stomach and practice speaking so that your hand moves when you breathe. If it doesn't, you probably sound more like Mickey Mouse than Charlton Heston. (If you are a woman, that's probably okay, but whether you are a man or woman, a deeper voice is better for "Bypassing No.")

If you think you are a "special case," then by all means, look into a voice coach, but you might want to work on your breathing first. I think you will be amazed at how much you can change the sound of your voice just by shifting your breathing.

There is another technique that can make your voice more effective and make you seem more intelligent at the same time. The degree to which you articulate will play a big role in how much of a genius (or not) other people think you are. The cleaner and crisper your words (up to a point), the smarter you will sound. Get some kind of recording device and record yourself saying something; read a few paragraphs aloud from a magazine, for example. Listen to determine whether your words sound like they were articulated cleanly, or, whether they sound a little muffled and rounded.

> **When you want to induce feelings like excitement, speak faster. When you need to calm and soothe your listener, slow down.**

If you find that you need to clean things up a bit, your tongue is where you will find the solution. The further forward in your mouth you move your tongue, the more articulation you will have, and the smarter you will sound. It's really just as simple as that.

In a poll taken to determine who had the best and worst sounding voices, the results confirmed our preference for low voices. James Earl Jones and Julia Roberts were voted the best speaking voices, while Fran Drescher and Gilbert Gottfried were voted the worst. I would invite you to find some clips of Jones and Roberts online, and spend some time listening to their voices, and notice how you feel. This will also provide your ears with something to model as you work on improving your own voice.

Let's talk about the speed and tempo of your speaking voice for a minute. Did you know that you could increase the heart rate of your audience just by talking faster? Likewise, you can slow their heart rate, by slowing your speaking rate and speed. When you want to induce feelings like excitement, speak faster. When you need to calm and soothe your listener, slow down.

Finally, it is critical to know the difference between an approachable voice and a trustworthy voice. Using only a trustworthy voice is going to make you come across as very dry, while using only an approachable voice will make you seem like a fun, but maybe not so knowledgeable person.

The approachable voice has lots of inflection and animation. It says, *"I'm fun, I'm safe, and I don't take myself too seriously."* This is the voice you want to use while building rapport and chit-chatting in general.

The trustworthy voice has less inflection and is accompanied by gestures that are more subdued. Each sentence should conclude with downward inflection to give more power and seriousness to them.

Neither of these voices is better than the other; they are both very important, but they need to be used at the right time.

"Bypassing No" will become much easier as you begin integrating these changes into your own speaking voice. Tackle them one at a time, and after one change has started to automate, add another. Before you know it, you will be using your voice much like a musician plays a finely tuned instrument.

Chapter 27:
It's Never a Good Idea to Tell
Someone "Your Idea is Stupid!"

"If once you forfeit the confidence of your fellow citizens, you can never regain their respect and esteem."

-Abraham Lincoln

The fact that you are reading this book tells me you are looking to become a better communicator and more skilled at "Bypassing No." It also tells me that you are probably not the kind of person who would look at a client or customer and say, *"Your idea is stupid!"*— not intentionally anyway. Nevertheless, that is exactly what we have done every time someone says something and we say *"Yes...BUT..."*

When we say *"Yes...but..."* we have just negated everything that came before the *"but."* For example, *"Yes, it is true that you have been coming in early for the last two weeks, and have stayed late most nights, BUT, we still need you to get all of your certifications up to date."* What they have heard is *"We don't care that you've come in early and stayed late. What we do care about is you having your certifications up to date!"*

This feels bad and can breed resentment. Once the feelings of resentment have festered, a "NO!" is close behind. Remember, we want to "Bypass No," and the way we do that does not come by making people resent us. It comes by validating them and their ideas.

Let's see how we can transform this statement by changing just one word. *"Yes, it is true that you have been coming in early for the last two weeks and have stayed late most nights, AND, what we need you to do now, is to get all of your certifications up to date"*

When we use "and" it makes whatever we say after the "and" seem like it is just an extension of what came before the "and."

> **Think back to the last time someone "yes butted" you. Were you open and relaxed, or, did you tense up a bit and feel resistant?**

This is actually so effective that you can completely disagree with someone, but still maintain a fair amount of rapport. Unfortunately, when you use "but," you can take something that you both agree on, make it seem like you do not respect their idea, and create a quarrel before you realize what has happened.

For example: there is a married couple who both love a particular steakhouse. While telling their friends about the restaurant one night the husband says, *"They have the best sirloin steaks anywhere!"* His wife adds, *"They do have good sirloins, BUT, the KC strips are heavenly!"*

Just beneath the surface, he may be feeling a bit slighted—as if she invalidated his statement—and it could change the course of the evening. Eventually, a pattern of this could even alter the course of their marriage. Let's see what happens with "and."

"They have the best sirloin steaks anywhere!" *"Yes, they do have good sirloins, AND, the KC strips are heavenly!"* He feels validated, and her comment about the KC strips just seems like a further promotion of his statement.

Bypassing 'No' In Business

Think back to the last time someone "yes butted" you. Were you open and relaxed, or, did you tense up a bit and feel resistant? Using "and" will keep things relaxed; using "but" closes things down.

The formula is very simple: *"Yes, and..."*

Start using this pattern in the next conversation you have, and watch how others glow when you validate them—even when you disagree with them. These two little words can alter the course of any conversation.

Bypassing 'No' In Business

.

Chapter 28:
Play "Dress Up" and "Eat up!"

"Clothes make the man. Naked people have little or no influence in society."

-Mark Twain

I saw the movie "Billy Jack" for the first time when I was about ten years old. Tom Laughlin directed and co-wrote the movie, as well as playing the main character, Billy Jack.

Billy Jack was a Native American Green Beret returning home from Vietnam. Well versed in hand-to-hand combat, Billy Jack thumps a motorcycle gang that had been harassing some Native American children. He fought, and easily beat, every one of the over-grown thugs in a show-down, using his bare hands.

To "be" Billy Jack required a few items: a black hat with headband, a Bald Eagle feather and an eagle talon (for its magical healing properties). I picked up a hat at a rummage sale and got both the feather and the talon I needed from a road-killed Red Tailed hawk. When I would get home from school, I would transform into "Billy Jack" by putting on my hat and snatching up my talon that I kept in a drawstring leather bag (my medicine bag).

After the transformation, I talked different, walked different, and most of all, I felt different. I was so much braver as "Billy Jack" and had far more confidence in my abilities. Once I put the hat and medicine bag away for the night, however, my confidence was put away with them. Most women can remember something similar when they played dress up with their mom's clothes and one of her old purses.

What does this have to do with "Bypassing No?" We feel differently when we dress differently and many studies show that we behave differently as well.

In an experiment where students were asked to take on the role of either a guard or a prisoner, those who dressed in the uniform of a guard became much more aggressive and rebellious. Those who dressed as an inmate became passive and displayed a beaten-down attitude.

You might remember when it was very popular in many companies to have "casual Friday." On this day, you could wear jeans and a polo shirt, for example, rather than the usual suit and tie. Most employees loved it and looked forward to the end of the week so they could dress "comfortably."

The owners of many of these companies, though, became less and less "comfortable" with "casual Fridays." Records showed a definite drop in productivity on the days people were dressing casually. Today, the term "casual Friday" has all but disappeared in many circles.

How do we explain the drop in productivity when dressing casually, or the aggressive behavior of the "guards" and passive behavior of the "prisoners?" It's all about the associations we have in our minds about the clothes we are wearing. When the associations we have are positive, we have greater feelings of self-respect and self-esteem. When the associations are less positive, feelings of self-respect and self-esteem decrease.

Key Point: When our feelings of self-respect and self-esteem are high, we are more likely to invest in ourselves and engage in behaviors that will contribute to our lives in a positive way.

In other words, the people you are talking to are going to, far more likely, say "Yes!" when they feel good about themselves. Since we know that most people feel better about themselves when they are dressed up, it makes sense to get them to put on their "Sunday best." But how?

It's easy. Combine dressing up with another powerful unconscious "good feeling" generator— FOOD. If the person you wish to influence usually wears L.L. Bean chino's and well aged T-shirts, invite them to dine with you somewhere where the standard attire is a couple of notches higher.

Just tell them *"Hey, I'd like to treat you to some of the best lobster bisque you've ever had in your life. It's a pretty "ritzy" place, so wear a jacket—maybe even a suit if you have one."* They will be thrilled to throw on some flashy duds for a free meal, and once they do, their feelings and behaviors will have shifted; they feel better, so you will more easily "Bypass No."

With clients I work with face-to-face on remedial issues (depression, grief, low self-esteem, etc.), I make it clear from the beginning that there are certain things I expect if I am going to work with them. If they are okay with my short list, we'll do it. If not, we will not.

One of the biggest things on my list is that there will be times when I ask them to do things that seem silly, or have no particular point, but must be done without question. I make it clear that I would never ask them to do something unsafe.

After one of their sessions, without telling them why, I will tell them to wear a suit and tie, or their best dress to their next appointment. I will video these "regular clothes" sessions and "dress up" sessions back–to-back. Later, I will have the client watch both videos and take note of the differences in their posture, gestures, facial expressions etc.

Many people are shocked at the difference. Clients that had been less than "highly receptive" in one session will be all ears and eyes in the next session, wearing a nice suit or dress, and feeling much better because of it.

Okay, let's get back to the FOOD. The desire for sex and food, are two of the most powerful drives on earth. For some, the desire for food may even be higher than the desire for sex. In any case, both are very intense.

We have lots of good feelings linked to food— or even the thought of food. Once we take our first bite of that piece of pie, or mouth-watering cheeseburger, a "brain cocktail" is mixed, and a cascade of "feel good" neurotransmitters flood our brain and body.

For example, chocolate can give us the same feelings we would otherwise get from the affection of another person. It contains *Pheyethylamine* (PEA), which is a drug that is one of the brains pleasure substances. In fact, scientists have called PEA a "love drug."

Chocolate is but one of dozens of foods that will radically alter someone's biochemistry and put them in a state that is far more conducive for getting "Yes" and "Bypassing No."

This strategy is so incredibly straightforward, it's embarrassingly simple:

Get someone to dress up nicer than they normally do, and then feed them. That's it.

Another benefit to taking them someplace nice, where you have a good excuse for asking them to dress up, is that the atmosphere will also exert a great deal of influence.

The quality tableware, well-dressed wait staff, soothing background music and even other diners will send strong unconscious signals of "You're worth it!" to your client or potential customer.

One more thing on food: if you schedule important meetings or sales presentations *after* lunch, STOP IT NOW! Healthy men and women are rarely closer to being "brain dead" than they are about an hour after lunch.

The "good" feelings have long since dissipated by the time they arrive for your appointment. Not only have you missed their peak "feel good" state, but also you are fighting a state that can rival drunkenness. Imagine "Joe" in two possible scenarios:

1. He sets an appointment for Mike to come in to his office after lunch. For lunch, Mike inhaled a double cheeseburger and fries and washed it down with a large soda. The only words he heard from the "wait staff" were "please pull around to the first window." Mike's wearing faded jeans and a T-shirt imprinted with, "Thank God, it's Friday."
2. Joe meets Mike at a steakhouse where a sports jacket is required. Mike walks in wearing pressed slacks, clean loafers and a handsome sports coat. They are both seated by someone who calls them "Sir."

Do you think there will be a BIG difference in how Mike thinks, behaves and feels from one example to the next? You had better believe it.

Bypassing 'No' In Business

"Bypassing No" isn't always about what you say or how you use your body; it can be something as simple as what someone is wearing, if they are eating, and if so, where?

Now you have a good excuse to start frequenting the nicest restaurants. Enjoy!

Chapter 29:
A Cocktail for Yes or No

"All I need is my brains, my eyes and my personality, for better or for worse."

-William Albert Allard

Remember the family gathering where you first met a particular uncle or aunt. You probably thought to yourself, "Man, they are really different than my mom or dad." They had different opinions, used different words, and had different behaviors than their own brothers or sisters.

You became aware of the cocktail mix we encounter everyday when dealing with people. Go to a liquor store and note how many different bottles of spirits are on the shelves. The same applies to people; their behaviors are as varied as the bottles on the shelf!

So what do you do? How do you sort out how to communicate and get a "yes" from so many different people? In order to "Bypass No," you will need to understand how they see the world differently than you do. Once you know this, you can adjust your communication to their style and connect with them more effectively.

The Tool:

Most people fit into one of four areas. If you can identify their major area, you will be able to adapt and connect far easier and quickly.

The acronym DISC signifies the four basic areas. We all exhibit one more significantly than the others.

The Dominant:

The D is for a Dominant type of person. They are fast paced, make decisions on very little information and tend to run the show. Often times they are perceived by others as overly aggressive, cold or distant, or egomaniacs. In reality, they simply want things done now. They are motivated by accomplishments and obtaining goals.

If you want to successfully "Bypass No" with a "D," be brief and to the point, never overload them with too much information, and always communicate what the outcomes will be. Allow them to feel in charge and ask their opinions. Words/phrases they often use include: results, outcomes, action, do for me, how quickly and is it done yet.

Jack is the Executive VP. During a meeting, he takes control and tends to drive his ideas. If an accountant brings in a 20-page report, Jack will say, *"Just give me the outcome on one page."*

The Influencer:

They are very focused on relationships and image. They are the life of the party as they flutter from one person to another. Highly persuasive and very likable, they know everyone and talk about everything. Others may perceive them as phony or unfocused as they jump from one issue to another. Challenged by organization, they tend to be late and overly active. Words they use include: I, fantastic, wonderful, unbelievable, fun and exciting.

To successfully "Bypass No" with an "I" be friendly and willing to listen to their stories. Building a relationship is the most important motivator they have and they will not compromise existing ones, even at the cost of a sale. They also want outcomes, but only as it relates to how it makes them look to others.

Jeff asks me to look at a new boat he wants to buy. I say, *"Why do you want it Jeff, isn't yours just fine?"* He says, *"It's got more style, it looks better and I like it better."* Typical "I" response.

The Steady:

The "S" is more steadfast. They are very people-oriented, but more focused on "We" versus "I." They want predictability, systems to follow, and tend to want more trust than others do. They are slower-paced than "D" or "I" but will get the job done right. The "S" does not like change or conflict and will avoid these if they can. Words/phrases they use will be trust, we, affect others and what support is provided.

"Bypassing No" with an "S" requires patience, being prepared, providing a system for change, and including others. Overly aggressive approaches will turn them off. Help them understand how it will help others. Always do what you say you will, or the trust will be broken.

June is upset. *"They've changed it again; why do they always change everything? It just puts more on us, and we can't keep up."*

The Competent:

The "C" is highly competent and detail oriented. If they have pocket protectors and carry spreadsheets, they are probably a "C." Their motivation is to avoid error, and they will be viewed as over-analyzers. Their pace is slower, and their decisions are based on risk avoidance. Words/phrases they use include: accuracy, the details are, how does this work, how do we avoid risk or what do the numbers tell us.

You can "Bypass No" with a "C" by having more information than needed. Knowledge and information equate to risk avoidance. Patience is required, as they have to process information before saying "yes." Also, be upfront with any negatives or defects in your offering; they will find it anyway!

I asked Jill a question, and she sits back to contemplate for a good 30 seconds. *"To ensure the accuracy, we would have to do it this way. I'm concerned about the President saying it will take too much time, but making a mistake of this proportion could be devastating."*

Summary:

This overview of the four basic behavioral types, should give you some insight into what sets them apart and how to adapt your communication with them.

All of the tools, ideas and techniques in this book will work with all the DISC types; you simply have to adapt them.

The key to making the DISC work for you is to observe the person's actions, words and environment.

1. Are they fast or slow paced?
2. Are they task or people oriented?
3. Are they motivated by results or relationships?
4. Are they motivated by accuracy or service?
5. Are they outgoing or more reserved?

By observing more, talking and pushing less, you will be able to "Bypass No" in no time.

More on the DISC @ http://www.AskHG.com/DISC